Th
GIBRALTAR

ROWLAND MEAD

GLOBETROTTER™

Second edition published in 2010
by New Holland Publishers (UK) Ltd
London • Cape Town • Sydney • Auckland

10 9 8 7 6 5 4 3 2 1

website: www.newhollandpublishers.com

Garfield House, 86 Edgware Road
London W2 2EA
United Kingdom

80 McKenzie Street
Cape Town 8001
South Africa

Unit 1, 66 Gibbes Street
Chatswood
NSW 2067, Australia

218 Lake Road
Northcote, Auckland
New Zealand

Distributed in the USA by
The Globe Pequot Press, Connecticut

This guidebook has been written by independent authors and updaters. The information
therein represents their impartial opinion, and
neither they nor the publishers accept payment
in return for including in the book or writing
more favourable reviews of any of the establishments. Whilst every effort has been made to
ensure that this guidebook is as accurate and up
to date as possible, please be aware that the
facts quoted are subject to change, particularly
the price of food, transport and accommodation. The Publisher accepts no responsibility or
liability for any loss, injury or inconvenience
incurred by readers or travellers using this guide.

Publishing Manager: Thea Grobbelaar
DTP Cartographic Manager: Genené Hart
Editors: Thea Grobbelaar, Alicha van Reenen
Designer: Nicole Bannister
Cartographers: Nicole Bannister, Tanja Spinola
Picture Researcher: Shavonne Govender

Reproduction by Resolution (Cape Town)
Printed and bound by Times Offset (M) Sdn. Bhd.,
Malaysia.

Front Cover: *An aerial view of the Rock.*
Title Page: *The lighthouse at Europa Point.*

CONTENTS

MAKE THE MOST OF YOUR GUIDE

Reading these two pages will help you to get the most out of your guide and save you time when using it. Sites discussed in the text are cross-referenced with the cover maps – for example, the reference 'Map D–C3' refers to the Gibraltar Area Map (Map D), column C, row 3. Use the Map Plan below to quickly locate the map you need.

MAP PLAN

Outside Back Cover   Outside Front Cover

Inside Front Cover   Inside Back Cover

THE BIGGER PICTURE

Key to Map Plan

A – Excursions

B – Costa de la Luz

C – Gibraltar Town Plan

D – Gibraltar Area

E – Ronda

F – Málaga

G – Tangier

USING THIS BOOK

Key to Symbols

⊠ — address

☎ — telephone

℘ — fax

🖳 — website

🖰 — e-mail address

🕘 — opening times

ᵟ — entry fee

🍽 — restaurants nearby

🚌 — tours

Map Legend

motorway	▬▬▬	main road	Queensway
national road	▬▬▬	other road	Main
main road	▬▬▬	mall	IRISH TOWN
minor road	▬▬▬	built-up area	
railway	▬▬▬	building of interest	National Archives
ferry route	– – –		
route number	9 3215	museum	■
city	GIBRALTAR	college	■
major town	⊙ Marbella	parking	P
town	O Estepona	shopping centre	Ⓢ El Corte Inglés
large village	◎ Tarifa	river	
village	O Casares	dam	Salinas
airport	✈ ✈	library	📖
cave	🕳	post office	⊠
dive site		tourist information	i
hotel	Ⓗ CANNON	place of worship	△ ▲ △ Church Mosque Synagogue
place of interest	★ Moorish Baths	police station	●
lighthouse	♁	bus terminus	🚍
viewpoint		gate	●–●
park & garden	Coach Park	hospital	⊕

Keep us Current

Travel information is apt to change, which is why we regularly update our guides. We'd be most grateful to receive feedback from you if you've noted something we should include in our updates. If you have any new information, please share it with us by writing to the Publishing Manager, Globetrotter, at the office nearest to you (addresses on the imprint page of this guide). The most significant contribution to each new edition will be rewarded with a free copy of the updated guide.

5

GIBRALTAR

Looming imperiously over the southern point of Spain, the Rock of Gibraltar celebrated its Tercentenary in 2004 – three hundred years of British rule full of incident, warfare and political intrigue. With its strategic position, guarding the Straits of Gibraltar, it has always been a bone of contention between neighbouring nations and the Rock is littered with defensive walls, bastions, cannons and other relics of conflict. Spain has always claimed Gibraltar as its own, but Britain insists that this is not up for negotiation, while the Gibraltarians wish to remain British, a desire regularly confirmed in referendums. In these days of modern warfare techniques, Gibraltar's location is no longer as strategic as it was, and since the British forces left the Rock in the hands of the locally recruited Royal Gibraltar Regiment in 1991, the ambience has changed considerably. Cruise liner passengers and tourists from the Costa del Sol have replaced British servicemen in the pubs and shops of Main Street and Gibraltar is striving to develop a new identity through offshore financial services and tourism.

Disraeli's Gibraltar

It is not widely known that Benjamin Disraeli, the 19th-century prime minister had close connections with Gibraltar. His early years gave no clue to his future eminence, as his initial novels failed and he was constantly in debt and often in ill health. A 'grand tour' was recommended and his first port of call was Gibraltar, where he was the guest of the governor, Sir George Don. Disraeli was at the height of his 'dandyism' and his foppish behaviour was the talk of the officers on the Rock. He used two canes, one for the day and one for the evening, changing with a flourish at the night gun. The evening *paseo*, was, of course, much to his liking. He used Gibraltar as a base for sallies into Andalucía and on one memorable occasion he was robbed by bandits en route to Ronda. His experiences, he claimed, did much to colour his future life.

The Land

The Rock is a huge block of Jurassic limestone, thrust up by a collision of the African and European plates. Movement has been considerable because marine fossils have been found on the highest parts of the Rock, which rises to 426m (1396ft). The steepest slopes face north and east, while most of the settlement is on the west side, extending by land reclamation into the Bay of Algeciras. Gibraltar and the mountains on the other side of the Straits in Morocco were known as the Twin Pillars of Hercules, but over geological history there has often been a land ridge connecting the two continents. During the Ice Age the Mediterranean drained more than once. When sea levels rose the waters of the Atlantic rushed back into the Mediterranean creating a huge waterfall, many times the size of Niagara, to the south of Gibraltar. During wetter climatic periods, rain seeping through the limestone of the rock dissolved much of the material, creating numerous caves and caverns. Into these caves, the dripping water re-deposited limestone, forming features such as stalactites, stalagmites and pillars, shown impressively in St Michael's Caves. Today, Gibraltar is some 6km (4 miles) long and 2km (1.2 miles) wide, joined to Spain in the north by alluvial land on which the airport is built.

> **Getting a Good Weather Forecast**
> As Gibraltar has its own microclimate, which is significantly different to the neighbouring Costas of Spain, it is often important to get a reliable weather forecast, particularly for outdoor activities such as sailing and diving. These forecasts have traditionally been supplied by the Met Office at RAF Gibraltar and are broadcast on BFBS Radio and Radio Gibraltar at regular intervals. You can call ☎ 200 53416 for regular updates.

Climate

Gibraltar experiences a Mediterranean climate typified by hot dry summers and mild wet winters. It is, however, milder, windier and wetter than the nearby Costa del Sol. In winter the prevailing wind is from the west and snow or frost is extremely rare. The mean temperature in January is 13.5°C (56.3°F). In summer, the Levante, an easterly wind, forces warm air to the top of the Rock where it cools, forming lenticular-shaped clouds, increasing humidity and shading the town. Maximum and minimum temperatures in the summer are 13°C (55.4°F) and 30°C (91.4°F) respectively, with around 10.5 hours of sunshine daily.

Opposite: *The settlement of Catalan Bay on the west side of the Rock, with the Caleta Palace Hotel dominating the scene.*
Below: *A view over the town and harbour from the top cable car station.*

OVERVIEW

Fauna and Flora
For those who take a special interest in environmental and n atural history matters, more information is available from GONHS (The Gibraltar Ornithological and Natural History Society) at ⌨ www.gonhs.org ☎ 350 72639, 📠 350 74022. Founded in 1976, the organization runs an observatory at Jew's Gate and holds rambles on the last Sunday of the month. Accommodation can be arranged at Lower Bruce's Farm Environmental Research Centre. The Society's excellent website has a full systematic list of the fauna and flora of Gibraltar.

Below: *The Upper Rock Nature Reserve has typical Mediterranean maquis vegetation.*

Flora and Fauna

The plant life of Gibraltar is similar to much of the coastal Mediterranean, with a few notable exceptions. The eastern and northern cliffs are too steep for much in the way of flora, while the gentler slopes on the lower eastern side of the Rock have largely been built over. The Upper Rock, however, is full of interest and is a designated nature reserve where over 600 plants have been identified. The vegetation is given the name of maquis and consists of a tall dense scrub dominated by the **rock rose,** with numerous low trees such as **umbrella pine**, **Aleppo pine**, **fig** and **kermes oak**. Herbal plants include **rosemary** and **thyme**, while there are 10 varieties of **orchid** to be seen. Spring, from February to May, is the best time to see the colourful flowers, which include **paper white narcissus**, **common asphodel**, **candytuft** and **giant squill**. Near Europa Point the cliffs are festooned with **Hottentot fig**. The flora of the Rock has to be tough to survive the dry alkaline soil, hot winds and summer drought.

Mammals are rare on Gibraltar, apart from several species of **bat** and the famous **Barbary apes** (*see* page 18). The bird life of Gibraltar attracts enthusiasts from all over Europe. There are a number of interesting resident birds, such as the **blue rock thrush, peregrine falcon** and **Barbary partridge**. Gibraltar is the only place on mainland Europe where the Barbary partridge can be found – an important piece of information for 'twitchers'. The main attraction for bird-watchers, however, is the spring and autumn migration of raptors and storks. These are soaring birds that cannot beat their wings for long distances. They must therefore seek the shortest sea crossing to and from Africa, which means passing over Gibraltar. At peak periods over 10,000 raptors may pass Gibraltar in a single day. **Honey buzzards**, **black kites**, **booted** and **short-toed eagles** and **griffon vultures** are among the

more spectacular migrants. Smaller songbirds can fly over water and deserts without stopping and therefore cross the Mediterranean on a much broader front. Many pass over Gibraltar, often at night, when they can be detected on radar screens. Hundreds of thousands of sea birds also commute between the Atlantic and the Mediterranean, passing close to Gibraltar. These include **shearwaters**, **gannets** and **terns**. The seas around Gibraltar also contain numerous families of dolphins (*see page 33*) and a number of boats take visitors to see these fascinating creatures.

Above: *Gibraltar is the only place in Europe where the Barbary partridge can be found.*

History in Brief

It is now known that Gibraltar was occupied by man during prehistoric times. A female skull found in a cave on the north face of the Rock has been dated as Neanderthal – this discovery pre-dated the finding of a male skull in the Neander Valley by eight years, but its significance was not realized at the time. Local guides like to point out to visitors that 'Neanderthal Man' should really be 'Gibraltar Woman'. The original skull is now in London's Natural History Museum, but a copy can be seen Gibraltar's Museum in Bomb House Lane (*see page 39*). Further important remains were found in Gorham's Cave near the southeast tip of the Rock in 1928. Here, flint artefacts and the bones of animals such as hyenas and deer were discovered,

Cork For The Bottle
The evergreen oak (*Quercus suber*) flourishes on the upper slopes of the Rock and in neighbouring Andalucía. The tree can live for up to 800 years and during this time its bark can be stripped on many occasions. Cork is best known as a stopper in wine bottles. In recent years, however, wine producers have been turning to artificial cork or screw tops. This has alarmed environmentalists, who fear that, because of lack of demand, the cork woods will be chopped down to make way for fields of sunflowers or wheat, types of land use that are far less attractive to wildlife.

dating from 100,000 years ago.

Phoenicians and ancient Greeks also left traces of their occupation. The Phoenicians, who knew the Rock as *Calpe*, founded the settlement of Carteia at the head of the Bay of Gibraltar. The area became a place of worship where sailors sacrificed to the gods before facing the terrors of the Atlantic.

Moorish influence began in AD711, when the governor of Tangier, Tarik ibn Ziyad, landed on the Rock, which he used as a bridgehead, assembling a force of 10,000 men to begin his conquest of Spain.

He named the Rock *Jebel Tarik* (Tarik's Mountain), which over time became *Gibraltar*. The settlement itself was founded in AD1160 by the Almohad Muslims led by Abd-al-Murrim, who built the Moorish Castle and the early defensive walls. Gibraltar stayed in Moorish hands until a surprise attack by the Spanish, led by Guzman el Bueno in 1390. Twenty-five years later it was regained by the Moors led by the Sultan of Fez, after a siege of four and a half months. The Catholic Monarchs Ferdinand and Isabella began a reconquest of the peninsula in the 15th century and the Moors were evicted from the Rock in 1492 by Spanish forces. They were to stay on the Rock for a further 240 years until the **War of Spanish Succession**.

The Start of British Influence

Although Britain initially supported the Spanish against the French, Gibraltar was taken by a combined Anglo-Dutch fleet in 1740. Most of the inhabitants of Gibraltar fled to the Campo of Gibraltar, where they settled in San Roque, fully expecting to return

Processions of a Different Kind
Visitors to Gibraltar and nearby Andalucía soon become used to processions of various types, but one kind that occurs in spring should be avoided like the plague. This is the line of furry caterpillars that can be seen in a nose-to-tail convoy crossing roads and tracks and climbing walls. These are the caterpillars of the **Processionary Caterpillar Moth** (*Thaumatopoea processionea*) and known in Spain and Gibraltar as *orugas*. Never touch these caterpillars – their hairs will cause a painful rash and, if disturbed, they give off a fine dust which can cause respiratory problems, even causing death in small children. If you go into a *farmacia* and ask for a remedy, be careful how you pronounce *oruga*. The similar sounding *arruga* is a wrinkle, and *crema para arrugas* will not cure a rash caused by caterpillars!

to the Rock. They never did. Meanwhile Britain gained formal sovereignty over the Rock in the **Treaty of Utrecht** in 1713. Spain did not take this lying down, however, and made numerous diplomatic and military attempts to regain Gibraltar. The Rock has endured numerous sieges during its history, but the most serious was the Great Siege, Spain's last attempt to capture Gibraltar by military means. The siege lasted for four years, from 1779 to 1783, and much of the town was destroyed. The four years of shared hardship and privation bonded together the various sectors of the population, which consisted of Genoese, English and Moroccan Jews (and later Spanish, Portuguese and Maltese), and helped to forge a Gibraltarian identity. It was during the Great Siege that the first defensive tunnels were dug on the north face of the Rock (see page 17).

During the 19th century, Gibraltar was able to develop in relative peace. It became an important naval base and **Admiral Nelson** used it as his HQ when he became Commander-in-Chief Mediterranean. Nelson was to perish at the Battle of Trafalgar (1805) and his body was taken in a cask of brandy to Rosia Bay, before being shipped back to England and interment at St Paul's Cathedral. At the same time as the Battle of Trafalgar a yellow fever epidemic raged in Gibraltar, killing over a third of the population. In 1830, Gibraltar was declared a Crown Colony and at the same time the Royal Gibraltar Police Force was established.

> **History in Action**
> Every Sunday morning the Rock's historical past is brought alive when a group of soldiers in 18th-century period uniform march at 12 noon from Bomb House Lane to Casemates Square. Here they enact a **Ceremony of the Keys** and then march back up Main Street to the Cathedral of St Mary the Crowned, replicating the march of British soldiers when they took Gibraltar in 1704.

Opposite: *This skull of a woman, dated as Neanderthal, was dicovered in a cave on the north face of the Rock.*
Below: *Gibraltar has many connections with the Battle of Trafalgar, as this memorial shows.*

Two World Wars

Gibraltar played a strategic role during the wars of the 20th century, particularly in World War II, when Hitler devised 'Operation Felix', a plan to invade the Rock, which fortunately never materialized. The civilian population, however, were evacuated to places such as Jamaica, Madeira and Great Britain. Ironically, those who came to London were in far greater danger than if they had stayed in Gibraltar. World War II also saw the construction of further tunnels in the Rock and many of these galleries became barracks for the 30,000 British troops who were stationed at Gibraltar. Other tunnels were used for storing guns and ammunition, so that Gibraltar became a formidable fortress guarding the western approaches to the Mediterranean. It was during World War II that Winston Churchill heard of a legend that if the Barbary apes ever died out, the British would give up the Rock. He therefore made sure that the apes' numbers were kept up by importing additional animals from Morocco. After the war, the civilians were speedily repatriated, the majority being back on the Rock by the end of 1946.

The postwar years were full of incident. General Franco made strenuous efforts to persuade Britain to give up the Rock and return it to Spain, but in a series of referendums the Gibraltarians always overwhelmingly voted to continue their association with Britain. Franco, incensed, closed the border in 1965 and it was to remain so for 14 years. In 1983 the border was opened for pedestrians only. With the death of Franco and Spain's entry into the Common Market, the border was re-opened fully in 1985. Controversy, however, continued. In 1988, the British SAS shot three suspected IRA terrorists at a Shell petrol station close the border and although there had been some collaboration with the Spanish police, the incident did nothing toimprove Anglo-Spanish relations. By the turn of the century, both the British and Spanish governments seemed willing to come to a mutually acceptable arrangement over Gibraltar, but then the inhabitants again showed in a referendum that they were unwilling to accept change, rejecting any proposals for joint sovereignty.

Above: *World War II guns at Princess Caroline Battery at the Military Heritage Centre.*

Government and Economy

Gibraltar is a Crown colony with internal self-government, with its constitution dating back to 1969. The British monarch is the official Head of State. The United Kingdom is responsible for defence, foreign affairs, financial stability and internal security. The Queen is represented by a Governor (and Commander-in-Chief). There are three main political parties: the **Gibraltar Liberal Party** (led by Joseph García); the **Gibraltar Social Democrats** or GSD (led by Peter Caruana); and the **Gibraltar Socialist Labour Party** or GSLP (led by Joe Bossano). The Chief Minister is Peter Caruana who was elected in 1996 and who has been re-elected for two further terms. Under him is a Council of Ministers appointed from the 15 elected members of the House of Assembly by the governor in consultation with the Chief Minister. The people of Gibraltar are now able to vote in European elections and are classified as part of Devon and Cornwall in England.

The Port and Shipping

Gibraltar has been forced to change in recent years from a naval to a commercial port. The Port of Gibraltar is administered by the Port Authority. It offers a range of marine services tailored for the modern shipping industry, including bunkering facilities, dry docks, a ship repair yard (Cammell Laird), modern facilities for yachts, cargo handling facilities, a cruise ship terminal and the supply of stores and provisions. There is a fine view of the port and its facilities from the Upper Rock.

The economy has changed drastically in recent years. The British armed services now have only a token presence on the Rock and security is in the hands of the locally recruited **Royal Gibraltar Regiment**. With the garrison gone, Gibraltar is seeking to re-invent itself, relying on tourism and finance to fuel its economy. The financial sector has had a bumpy ride with accusations of money laundering and the crash of BCCI (Bank of Credit and Commerce International), when many expats on the Costa del Sol lost their life savings. Gibraltar is, nevertheless, an important offshore centre and by 1993 some 19 banks had branches on the Rock. Tourism is thriving, with around eight million visitors a year, many from cruise ships. Other important sectors are telecommunications and shipping. Gibraltar enjoys full employment and relies on foreigners for much of the menial work.

The People

Gibraltar has a population of 28,000, coming from a variety of ethnic groups including Spanish, Italian (Genoese), English, Maltese, Portuguese, German and Moroccan. Roman Catholicism is the predominant religion (78%). Others include Anglican and non-conformist (10%), Jewish (2%), Muslim (4%) and Hindu (2%). English is the official language though Spanish is widely used. Many people speak both languages in a dialect called *llanito* – the Spanish refer to the Gibraltarians as llanitos. English is taught in schools and English public examinations are taken. The government provides scholarships for students to attend English universities.

Below: *The Gibraltar flag is an elongated banner featuring the Arms of Gibraltar.*

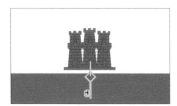

Architecture

Gibraltar has a curious mixture of architecture, reflecting its long history, turbulent past and military associations. The oldest structures are those of Moorish origin, including the Moorish Castle with its prominent Tower of Homage, some surviving defensive walls and the Moorish Baths in the basement of the Gibraltar Museum. The Roman Catholic cathedral in Main Street was built on the site of a mosque and some of its remains can still be seen. The original Moorish settlement was demolished and is now largely occupied by the Casemates Square area. Many older buildings were destroyed during the Great Siege. Of what remains, the Spanish architectural influence can be seen everywhere, with balconies often having ornate wrought-iron work, and interior courtyards. A good example of early Georgian architecture can be seen at the Garrison Library. Later styles can be seen at the Convent (the Governor's residence), which was itself built on the site of a 16th-century Franciscan monastery of which the old colonnade still remains. Elsewhere, the buildings reflect Gibraltar's role as a garrison, with stout defensive walls, bastions and grim barracks. With the departure of the military, many of the barracks have been converted into private apartments. Indeed, the overwhelming majority of Gibraltarians are flat-dwellers – there is simply no space for detached houses and gardens. In recent years a considerable amount of land has been reclaimed from the Bay of Gibraltar and modern architecture has been allowed full scope. Lively marinas, tall apartment blocks, an impressive new hospital and a new cruise liner terminal now grace the shoreline.

Above: *The Cathedral of the Holy Trinity has a surprising external architectural style with Moorish arches dominating.*

Dire Straits
Vast numbers of Moroccans have the ambition to live and work in the EU and many attempt to cross the Straits of Gibraltar illegally. They cross these treacherous waters in small open boats known as *pateras*. The boat owners exploit the would-be immigrants, often taking their life savings for the crossing. Many boats sink, however, and the local authorities estimate that the bodies of over 1000 illegal immigrants have been washed up on the shores of the Costa de la Luz during the last ten years. Those who do survive and evade the police face an uncertain future, being confined to low-paid work.

See Map D–E3 ★ ★ ★

Cable Car
The Cable car runs daily ☉ from 09:30. The time of the last car down depends on the season.
🎟 Variety of tickets available. Some include entry to attractions or a meal in the Upper Station restaurant. The ticket includes a multi-media presentation in a variety of languages, obtainable at the Upper Station. Note that the cable car may not run in bad weather conditions, particularly if it is windy. Concessions, but no credit cards.
☎ 200 77826.

CABLE CAR TO THE TOP OF THE ROCK

For most visitors a trip to the top of the Rock by cable car is an essential experience. The cable car leaves from the Lower Station in Rosia Road close to the Gibraltar Botanical Gardens and the Hotel Bristol, with a convenient car park nearby. As the cable car rises to the summit, superb views are revealed of the town, including the modern area built on land reclaimed from the sea. Details of the harbour show the dry docks and repair yards. With luck, a cruise liner or a nuclear submarine may be spotted. Way to the west is the Bay of Gibraltar, usually full of oil tankers waiting to berth at the nearby oil refinery. On the far side of the bay, backed by mountains, is the Spanish town of Algeciras. To the south, on a clear day, across the Straits of Gibraltar, the Atlas Mountains of Morocco and the towns of Ceuta and Tangier can be picked out. The cable car stops at the Middle Station, giving access to the **Apes' Den** and **St Michael's Caves**, and then proceeds to the Upper Station. From the viewing platform it is possible to look down onto the precipitous eastern side of the Rock, with its huge water catchments. The Mediterranean Sea and the Costa del Sol stretch away into the distance.

Below: *A cable car makes its way to the top of the Rock, giving superb views over the town.*

🌀 *See* Map D–H4	★ ★ ★

THE GREAT SIEGE TUNNELS

There are some 50km (30 miles) of tunnels in the Rock and the Great Siege Tunnels (a.k.a. Upper Galleries) are by far the most impressive. They are to be found on the north face of the Rock and entry is included in the **Official Rock**

Tour. The tunnels were excavated during the Great Siege of 1779–83 by the company of Soldier Artificers (the forerunners of the Royal Engineers). The garrison commander, General Elliot, offered a reward to anyone suggesting a way of mounting a gun on a projection on the north face of the Rock. A Sergeant Major Ince suggested excavating a gallery. As work progressed, ventilation holes were blasted and it was soon realized that these would make excellent gun emplacements. The 24-pounder cannons fitted on depressing gun carriages invented by a Lt. Koehler could fire northwards over the isthmus down towards Spanish lines ensuring the impregnability of the Rock. Examples of Koehler's gun carriage can be seen in St George's Hall and another in Casemates Square. Today, a tour of the tunnels shows a fascinating glimpse of life during the Great Siege. There are models of soldiers in the uniform of the time, including Sergeant Major Ince and General Elliot, plus plenty of real cannons. One cavern shows a diorama of an alleged banquet when Lord Napier entertained President Ulysses Grant of the USA to dinner in 1878.

Above: *The entrance to the Great Siege Tunnels on the north face of the Rock.*

The Great Siege Tunnels
🕐 Mon–Sat 10:00–19:00 in summer and 10:00–17:30 in winter
☎ 200 70052 (Rock Taxi Tours)
🛗 Included in Official Rock Tour
🍽 Snacks available

Above: *The Barbary apes are one of Gibraltar's most popular tourist attractions.*

⊛ *See* Map D–E4 ★ ★ ★

THE BARBARY APES

Gibraltar's famous Barbary apes, (*Macaca sylvanus*) are in fact a species of tailless monkey or macaque, the only ones on the mainland of Europe. They are natives of the Moroccan Atlas Mountains and legend has it that they came across from that country at a time when there was a land ridge between the two countries. However, the lack of prehistoric remains in the caves of Gibraltar would seem to discount this theory. The truth is that their presence in Gibraltar dates from the earliest days of the British garrison when they were introduced as pets by the soldiers. Inevitably, many escaped and found it easy to live in the wild.

Today the apes are thriving. There are around 250, living in five packs. They are no longer looked after by the British forces, the responsibility having been passed on to local environmental groups. Visitors are most likely to see the apes at the so-called **Apes' Den**, but there are usually plenty around at the upper station of the cable car. Although highly photogenic and playful, they can bite and are not as lovable as they look. Guard your camera and other valuables, which they take great delight in stealing. As their numbers have grown, the apes have become something of a problem, damaging vegetation, raiding dustbins and even attacking old ladies carrying groceries. Some culling is inevitable. The good news, however, is that a £2million improvement plan for the Upper Rock will include a new 'Apes' Den' with pools and climbing frames.

Don't Feed the Apes
There are notices all around the Upper Rock asking people not to feed the apes, with a hefty fine as a punishment. Sadly, this request is widely ignored by taxi drivers who give the animals peanuts and encourage their passengers to do the same. Visitors should, however, obey the rules. The apes are provided with plenty of nutritious food by their keepers.

St Michael's Caves

⊛ See Map D–D4   ★ ★ ★

ST MICHAEL'S CAVES

Gibraltar is composed of Jurassic limestone some 200 million years old. Rainwater picks up carbon dioxide and becomes slightly acidic, which reacts with calcite in the limestone, eventually dissolving the rock along its joints and bedding planes. Limestone areas, therefore, can be riddled with caves and caverns. There are reckoned to be nearly 150 natural caves on the Rock of Gibraltar and the most spectacular of these is the complex known as St Michael's Caves. The Upper Level is open to visitors and the entrance fee can be part of the Official Rock tour or the cable car fee. The cave has all the usual features such as stalactites, stalagmites, pillars and flow structures, all imaginatively lit. There are daily shows of *Son et Lumiere*. Look out for the stalagmite which has fallen on its side revealing a cross section showing the history of its growth. During World War II the caves were prepared as an emergency hospital, but fortunately never used. Today, the main cavern, with its marvellous acoustics, functions as a concert hall for music, opera and drama. There are also small dioramas with full-sized models of both Neanderthal and Neolithic man. Beneath the main cave, narrow passages lead to the Lower Level. Entrance is by pre-appointments and a special guide is needed, with groups restricted to 5–10 people and no children under 10. Helmets are provided and there is some abseiling and shinning up and down ropes.

St Michael's Caves
⊠ St Michael's Road, Upper Level
🕐 daily 10:00–17:30 in winter and 10:00–18:30 in summer
💰 Admission charge, but free with a cable car or Official Rock Taxi Tour ticket.
Lower Level: entry by prior arrangement. Contact the main Tourist Office,
☎ 200 45000

Below: *The concert hall in St Michael's Caves, noted for its excellent acoustics.*

See Map D–A4   ★ ★ ★

**Features of
Limestone Caves**
Water percolating
through limestone is
naturally rich in lime,
which it has dissolved
from the rock. When it
drips from the roof of
caves or caverns the
lime is re-deposited to
form stalactites which
hang from the roof and
stalagmites which build
up from the ground.
Sometimes they join up
to form pillars, which
may have a 'barley
sugar' appearance.
Other deposits take the
form of flow structures
on the walls of caves.
In many cases the re-
deposited material is
tinged by minerals in
the rock. Copper can
colour the rock green
or blue while iron
stains the rock red or
brown. It is clear that
the re-deposition fea-
tures in St Michael's
Cave are 'dead' – they
are no longer growing
in size and were
formed in wetter
geological times.

EUROPA POINT

The southern tip of Gibraltar is known as Europa Point. There is a viewing platform making a splendid spot to observe sea birds, dolphins, shipping in the Straits and the distant mountains of Morocco. On the top of low cliffs is the **Gibraltar Lighthouse**, claimed to be the only one outside Britain to be regulated by Trinity House. Dating from 1841, it rises to 49m (162ft) and is an important navigational signal for ships passing through the Straits. It has been automated since 1994. It is surrounded by the remains of old gun emplacements, amongst which is a shop, claiming to be the 'last in Europe'. North of the lighthouse is a gently sloping area (probably an old wave-cut platform) on which cricket is played. Rivalling the lighthouse as the dominant feature of Europa Point is the minaret of the **Ibrahim-al-Ibrahim Mosque**. The mosque was a gift from King Fahd of Saudi Arabia. Nearby is the **Shrine of Our Lady of Europa**. This chapel was built on the site of a Moorish mosque after the Spanish Reconquista in 1462. A permanent light was kept burning before the image of Our Lady of Europa, a 15th-century statue of the Virgin and child. The shrine was sacked by the pirate Barbarossa in 1540 and by the British in 1704. The statue was recovered from Algeciras in 1864. To the west of the shrine is a fragment of old Moorish pavement, while to the north is an old whipping post. There is a small **museum** recounting the history of the building. Europe Day (5 May) is celebrated with a pilgrimage to the shrine. Europa Point is the most southerly point of mainland Europe.

🌐 *See* Map D–G5   ★ ★ ★

THE EASTERN SIDE OF THE ROCK

Although rarely visited by tourists, the eastern side of the Rock is not without interest and is popular with locals, especially at weekends, when its beaches can be crowded. Access the eastern side from the first round-about after crossing the airport runway. Pass along Devil's Tower Road, named after an old observation tower, since demolished. This road continues to Europa Point (so that it is possible to circumnavigate the Rock) but the route is often closed due to rock falls in one of the many tunnels. Initially the route is disappointing, passing through a factory area, but the attractive beach of **Catalan Bay** is soon reached. There is much dispute about the origin of the name 'Catalan', but it seems certain that the inhabitants did not come from Catalonia, but rather from Genoa. The settlement has traditionally been a fishing village and there are a number of excellent seafood restaurants on the waterfront. Sitting on a headland on the south side of Catalan Bay is the cubist-looking Caleta Hotel (*caleta* means small bay in Spanish), which is popular with wedding groups.

Further south is **Sandy Bay**, backed by self-catering apartments and retirement homes. Further development on the eastern side is prevented by lack of space and the loss of afternoon sun. Looming over these settlements is the steep eastern face of the Rock with its landmark Water Catchments.

Above: *The Caleta Hotel dominates Catalan Bay on the eastern side of the Rock.*
Opposite: *Europa Point with its prominent lighthouse.*

<u>The Shrine and Museum of Our Lady of Europa</u>
🕐 10:00–13:00 and 14:00–19:00 Mon–Fri. 11:00–13:00 and 14:00–19:00 Sat, Sun and holidays.
☎ 200 71230

Above: *The Sunken Garden (the Dell) in the Botanical Gardens is a favourite location for weddings.*

The Botanical Gardens
✉ Europa Road
🕐 Open daily 08:00–sunset
♿ Admission free

The Moorish Baths
✉ in the Gibraltar Museum, 18–20 Bomb House Lane
☎ 200 74289
🖥 www.gib.gi/museum
🕐 Open 10:00–18:00 Mon–Fri, 10:00–14:00 Sat
♿ Entrance fee (with concessions, no credit cards) covers a tour of the baths.

See Map D–E4 ★★★

THE BOTANICAL GARDENS

Formerly known as the Alameda Gardens (*alameda* is the Spanish word for a tree-lined promenade), they were the brainchild of Governor Sir George Don, who raised the money for their formation by a series of lotteries and by docking a day's pay from every soldier serving on the Rock. Sandwiched between the Rock Hotel and the casino to the east, the cable car park to the north and the docks to the west, the Botanical Gardens provide a haven of peace amongst the hustle and bustle of the town. The gardens were opened in April 1816 at the side of a parade ground, which was also the spot where mutineers were hanged. After a period of neglect, the gardens were revitalized in the 1990s, helped by some specimen plants sent from Kew Gardens in London. Entry is through wrought-iron gates dedicated to Governor Don. Some of the trees in the gardens are over 200 years old and, as well as Gibraltar plant specimens, there are flowers and shrubs from all over the world, particularly those with a similar climate such as the Cape area of South Africa, Perth in Western Australia, the Canary Islands and Madeira. Cacti, succulents, palms and dragon trees are particularly impressive. In the far corner of the gardens is a small wildlife park, with a number of animals and birds confiscated by customs from illegal traders (*see page 35*). A dell with a pond and waterfall is popular with wedding parties, while an open-air theatre is used in the summer for concerts and other events.

THE MOORISH BATHS

🌀 *See* Map C–E5   ★ ★ ★

THE MOORISH BATHS

The baths are located at Gibraltar Museum (*see* page 28) and lie partly under this building and the neighbouring Ordnance House. It is believed that the baths date from around 1335. The main hall of the baths was thought to have originally been twice the present size, but was partly destroyed during the Great Siege in 1779. It has a central dome with six arches supported on differing columns, including 4 half-brick columns, 3 columns of polished stone and one brick freestanding column believed to be a later addition. Four capitals on the pillars are of Visigoth origin, while one is Roman. This mixed bag was probably brought in from other sites in the vicinity. The main hall probably had vestibules separated by curtains where bathers could undress and relax. Each cubicle was lit by natural light filtering from star-shaped openings above. The cold room has higher ceilings to retain the cooler temperatures and contained shallow cold baths. The hot room is entered through a large round arch. It is believed that the steam bath was located at the north end and the hot plunge bath on the southern side. Under-floor ducts can clearly be seen and hot air would have been pumped through from the boiler room next door. Conservation work in the 1970s aggravated the original brickwork by using Portland cement – this was impermeable and built up damp.

The Moorish Baths are reckoned to be the best-preserved in the Iberian Peninsula and should not be missed.

Bathing the Moorish Way

Bathing for the Moors was not just for pleasure or hygiene, but part of the religious practice known as *hamman*. Entry to the baths was through an open-air courtyard and then into the entrance hall, where the visitor was welcomed and the moved into separate areas for men and women. There were three rooms – the cold, the warm and the hot. The cold room was for undressing. The warm and hot rooms, with their pools, had high humidity causing perspiration in order to clean out the pores. At the side of the pools were rest areas where it was possible to have a haircut or massage. The baths were places for lounging, relaxation, gossip and doing business.

Below: *Elegant arches support the different columns of the Moorish Baths.*

**Nelson's Anchorage
(for 100-ton gun)**
✉ Rosia Road
🕐 Open 09:30–17:15
Mon–Sat
💰 Small admission
charge.

Parson's Lodge
✉ Rosia Road
🕐 Open 10:00–18:00
Mon–Sat
💰 Small admission
charge.

⊙ *See Map C–H4* | ★ ★ ★

MAIN STREET

Undoubtedly the most popular location on the Rock for day visitors, Main Street stretches from Southport Gate in the south to Casemates Square in the north. It is largely pedestrianized and usually thronged with shoppers. The attraction is clear. **Shops** range from British institutions like Marks and Spencer, to Indian bazaars, American fast-food takeaways, high-class jewellers and shops selling duty-free alcohol and cigarettes. Add some typical English **pubs** and a variety of **restaurants** and there is plenty of interest for everyone. Apart from the shops, there are other places of interest. The **Convent**, now the Governor's residence, is at the upper end of Main Street. Take a beer in the Angry Friar pub opposite and watch the changing of the guard. Nearby is the **John Mackintosh Hall**, a venue for concerts and art exhibitions. Also nearby are the **Law Courts**, fronted by a luxuriant garden. Further south, on the east side of Main Street is the imposing Roman Catholic **Cathedral of St Mary the Crowned**, built on the site of a Moorish mosque. On the opposite side of the street is **John Mackintosh Square**, flanked by the **City Hall**, the **House of Assembly** and numerous cafés. Just to the west of Main Street is the area known as **Irish Town**, home of the Rock's original **Police Station** (now moved further south). Don't miss the **Post Office**, which is also the home of the Gibraltar Philatelic Bureau (there is another branch in the Watergardens). Main Street also has several banks and currency exchange facilities.

Below: *The House of Assembly, one of many buildings flanking John Mackintosh Square.*

See Map D–C3 | ★ ★ ★

ROSIA BAY AND THE 100-TON GUN

Rosia Bay, on the west side of the Rock, is Gibraltar's only natural harbour and it was here that *HMS Victory* came with Admiral

Nelson's body after the Battle of Trafalgar (1805). The bay is protected by low cliffs on which is the Napier Battery, named after Baron Napier of Magdala, who was governor of Gibraltar from 1876 to 1882. The whole area is full of military history and wartime relics. Find time to visit **Parson's Lodge**, a complex of gun positions, shell stores, batteries, shell hoists and magazines. On the north side of Rosia Bay is the extraordinary 100-ton gun. Two of these 'superguns' were made for the Italian navy, whereupon the British military authorities began to worry about their own defences. Four more guns were made, two for Malta and two for Gibraltar. The guns were designed by Sir William Armstrong in 1871 and the 100-ton gun on show was installed in 1882. It was said to take between 2 and 3 hours to get the gun ready for firing. It is reputed that the 35 artillerymen working on the gun were so good at their job and the gun so accurate that they could hit a single goose in a flock at 7000 yards! The gun could fire one round every four minutes and the 2000lb shell had a range of eight miles. The battery was also a position for four 3.7 anti-aircraft guns during World War II and two of these guns are visible today, one on the top of the left flank of the battery and the other directly in front of the 100-ton gun.

Above: *The 100-ton gun at Rosia Bay. The gun was designed by William Armstrong to defend the Straits.*

> **Victorian Supergun**
> There are many stories and myths about the 100-ton gun. It came out from Britain on the *SS Stanley* and was winched out of the ship by 60 men, but as the gun rose so did the ship, making it impossible to transfer it to the waiting barge. A hundred tons of ballast including a number of soldiers was needed before the transfer could be effected. It then took 20 days to move the gun (the weight of two Chieftain tanks), on a sleigh, 400yd to its present position. Then there is the story of the round that failed to fire. An officer called for a volunteer to crawl down the barrel and attach a rope to the shell. After a long pause a man eventually stepped forward. At the completion of the task he was made a Lance Bombardier on the spot.

Above: *The Land-port Gate is the main entrance to Casemates Square and Main Street.*

Koehler Depression Gun Carriage
In the centre of Casemates Square is an example of the Koehler Depression Gun Carriage. Lt. Koehler of the Royal Artillery is said to have designed the carriage so that cannonballs could be fired down on the Spaniards from the Upper Galleries during the Great Siege. Recent research, however, suggests that these gun carriages were being used in Germany before this time. Possibly Koehler had seen these and later claimed the design for his own. Other ex-amples of the carriage can be seen in the Great Siege Tunnels.

See Map C–A4   ★ ★ ★

CASEMATES SQUARE

Visitors arriving at Gibraltar on foot cross the airport runway and arrive at the city's walls. The **Landport Gate** (with a working drawbridge) leads into the attractive and vibrant Casemates Square. An alternative entry is via **Casemates Gate** from Line Wall Road. The Square has a long and chequered history, with many military connections. It gets its name from the former **British Barracks** located in the north of the Square, but its origins go back to Moorish times, when Hassan took over Gibraltar. It became a residential district named La Barcina, where people lived in single-storey houses in the Berber style. In Spanish times it was part of the Villavieja (or old town). It was then taken over by the British, but the settlement was largely destroyed during the Great Siege, so it was levelled and became a military parade ground. It was also used for public hangings. Today, Casemates Square shows the Medi-terranean face of Gibraltar, with outdoor cafés, tapas bars and other meeting places, shops and a tourist information office. A small shopping arcade is full of craft shops selling jewellery, silverware and Moroccan goods. Don't miss the **Gibraltar Glassworks** where you can stand on a platform to see the glassblowers at work (if the crowds are too great you can watch the proceedings on video). Their masterpieces are for sale at the shop. Note the statue of a soldier, unveiled by the chief minister in 2004 and dedicated to the men of the Gibraltar Regiment.

THE CONVENT

See Map C–G4 ★★

THE CONVENT

The Convent, located in the southern end of the Main Street, is the official home of the Governor of Gibraltar. It was originally a Franciscan Monastery. The friars had been in Gibraltar for over 40 years before building the monastery between 1430 and 1440. After the British took over the Rock, the Convent became the residence of the senior British officer, who shared it with the friars. They were eventually expelled in 1714. The British took over the monastery's chapel at the same time, naming it the King's Chapel. The Convent is an imposing brick and stone building in Gothic style with two prominent 'Dutch Ends' and a square Portland stone doorway with roof. The nave of the chapel now forms the ballroom and the 16th-century cloisters remain intact. The Convent was expanded in 1864 with construction of a banquet hall, which displays the coats of arms of various governors. The panelling is also of interest, being made from cedar washed ashore form the wrecks of Spanish boats sunk in the Grand Attack of 1782. The patio has a statue of General Elliot, believed to have been carved from the bowsprit of a Spanish galleon captured at the Battle of Trafalgar. Behind the Convent is an attractive garden, containing many specimen trees planted by visiting dignitaries, including King Edward VII, the Japanese Crown Prince Hirohito and Queen Elizabeth II. A venerable dragon tree is thought to be over 500 years old.

A Haunting Tale
It is claimed that the Convent is haunted by a Grey Lady. She was a nun who eloped with her lover, a Franciscan monk. They fled by rowing boat across the bay towards Algeciras, but were unfortunately caught in a storm. The monk was drowned, but the nun survived, eventually being caught and returned to the Convent where she was executed.

Below: *The Convent, in the Main Street, is the official residence of the Governor of Gibraltar.*

See Map C–E5   ★★

Gibraltar Museum
✉ Bomb House Lane, Gibraltar
☎ 200 74289
🕐 Open Mon–Fri 10:00–18:00, Sat 10:00–14:00
💰 Entrance fee.
🍽 There is a small café and shop.
(NB There are plans to move the museum to Casemates Square some time in the future.)

GIBRALTAR MUSEUM

The museum is located in a 14th-century reconstructed building that was once used as officers' quarters. It was inaugurated in 1930 by the governor Sir Alexander Godley and no doubt chosen as the place for a museum because of the Moorish Baths lying underneath the site (see page 23). Entry is through a shady courtyard with café chairs and tables. After paying the entrance fee, proceed to a room where an informative audiovisual presentation takes place every 15 minutes stressing Gibraltar's natural and human history. The museum is a mixture of traditional and modern displays. Inevitably a number of rooms are given over to the Rock's military history, with coats-of-arms, flags and weaponry. One section is devoted to the Great Siege of 1779–83. There are interesting areas on the archaeology, geology and natural history of Gibraltar. One of the most impressive rooms consists of a mock-up of archaeologists excavating Gorham's Cave, the site of the discovery of numerous pre-Roman artefacts. The museum's most important archaeological exhibit is now in London's Natural History Museum. This is the female skull discovered in Forbes Quarry on the north face of the Rock in 1848. Its significance was not realized at the time, but modern dating techniques have revealed that it is of Neanderthal age. Don't miss the enormous model of Gibraltar as it was in 1850.

Below: The Gibraltar Museum is housed in a 14th-century building located over the Moorish Baths.

Left: *The entrance to Trafalgar Cemetery, a shady spot at the south end of Main Street.*

TRAFALGAR CEMETERY

The southern end of Main Street is marked by Charles V Wall. Through it are cut the Southport and Referendum Gates, the latter to commemorate the 1967 referendum, which confirmed the Gibraltarians' resolve to remain tied to Britain. Just past Southport Gate lies the Trafalgar Cemetery, with its close links to Admiral Horatio Nelson. In October 1805, one of history's greatest sea battles was fought off Trafalgar Point, a few miles north of Gibraltar. Despite a victory for Britain, Admiral Nelson was killed in the battle aboard *HMS Victory*. The majority of the sailors killed in the action were buried at sea, but two were interred in the Trafalgar Cemetery, along with others who died in the naval action off Algeciras between the French and British fleets in 1801. Other gravestones indicate victims of the yellow fever epidemics of 1804, 1813 and 1814. The association of the graveyard with the Battle of Trafalgar does not seem to have been realized until many years after the event. Nelson's body, meanwhile, was pickled in a barrel of brandy, before being brought ashore at Rosia Bay.

> ### The Other Admirals
> It is well known that Admiral Nelson was the hero of the Battle of Trafalgar, despite his death. But what happed to the commanders of the French and Spanish fleets? The French Admiral Pierre Villeneuve suffered a fate worse than death, in that he lost not just the battle, but his honour. He was captured by the British, but allowed to return home to France, where, unable to face humiliation and the derision of Napoleon, he stabbed himself in the heart. The Spanish Commander Federico Carlos Gravina had been involved in the Great Siege of Gibraltar and was a highly regarded sailor and diplomat. Gravina survived the battle and fled in his flagship the *Principe de Asturias* to the port of Cádiz. He was seriously wounded, however, and gangrene set in. He died painfully five months later and is buried in San Fernando, just outside Cádiz.

HIGHLIGHTS

Above: *John Mackintosh Square is the focus of much of the life of Gibraltar.*

Local Boy Makes Good

John Mackintosh was born in Gibraltar in 1865. He spent much of his youth in London, where he developed his business acumen. On his return to Gibraltar, he joined forces with his uncle to run a company dealing in shipping and cotton goods. He then made a considerable amount of money in the coal business, before forming the Calpean Shipping Company, building three cargo ships during the 1930s. His business interests then turned to gas supply. Mackintosh died in 1940 at the age of 74. He provided in his will the funds to build the John Mackintosh Hall at the southern end of Main Street.

See Map C–C4	★★

JOHN MACKINTOSH SQUARE

Located in the central area of Main Street, the John Mackintosh Square has enjoyed a number of names during Gibraltar's history. Always an open square, it was known in Spanish times as La Gran Piazza. When the British took over the Rock they called it Grand Parade. Other descriptions include the Alameda, El Martillo and the Jews' Market. It gained its present name of John Mackintosh Square in 1940 after the death of the local businessman and benefactor who made his money in shipping and cotton goods. Look out for Mackintosh's bust on the west end of the square. There is a hotchpotch of buildings around the Square. Dominating the west side is the **City Hall**, which houses Gibraltar's City Council and the Mayor's Parlour. Built in 1815 on the site of an old hermitage, the City Hall has had a chequered career, being at various times a hotel, a parcels office and the residence of the Duke of Connaught, the son of Queen Victoria. On the east side of the Square stands the **House of Assembly**, Gibraltar's parliament building. Governor Sir George Don laid the foundation stone of the building in 1817 – look for his bust overlooking Main Street – and it was purpose-built as a library with funds raised by local merchants and public subscription (the subscribers' names are on a marble slab in the lobby of the building). The building was used by the Legislative Council in 1950 and became the House of Assembly in 1969. There are numerous eateries around the square.

See Map D–I3 ★★

GIBRALTAR'S MARINAS

Gibraltar's three marinas provide all the facilities that yachtsmen require, such as permanent and visitors' berths, haul-out facilities, hook ups for sewerage, water and electricity, repair services, chandlers and restaurants. The marinas, however, are not just for the sailing fraternity, providing many activities for the visiting tourist. They have some of the best restaurants in Gibraltar and provide most of the Rock's nightlife. The marinas are the starting point for some active leisure pursuits, such as diving, canoeing, sport fishing and dolphin-watching, while sailing schools provide instruction for the aspiring sailor in the sheltered waters of Gibraltar Bay. The areas around the newer marinas have some high-quality apartments, both for permanent residents and as holiday lets.

Gibraltar's oldest marina is **Sheppard's**, which was founded in 1961 with extensive boatbuilding and repair facilities. It has berths for 150 yachts and looks out over the airport runway. Nearby is **Marina Bay**, which opened in 1979. Apart from the usual facilities for yachtsmen, Marina Bay provides a health clinic, a large supermarket and some excellent international restaurants. Gibraltar's most recent marina development is the **Queensway Quay**, located at the historic Ragged Staff Wharf. The marina, which opened in 1994, is hemmed in by some of the most ex-clusive Mediterranean-style residential developments in Gibraltar.

Historic Wharf
Ragged Staff Wharf is reputed to be the old-est boat landing point in Gibraltar. It was developed by the British to victual their ships and later became the traditional landing place for new Governors and visiting dignitaries. The steps leading up from the wharf became known as Governor's Steps – a fact recorded on the plaque at the top of the steps.

Marinas
Sheppard's
☎ 200 75148
Marina Bay
☎ 200 73300
Queensway Quay
☎ 200 75148

Below: *The Queensway Marina provides all the services required by yachtsmen, plus some of the best restaurants in town.*

See Map D–H3 | ★★

The American War Memorial
Halfway along Line Wall is the American War Memorial, which was unveiled in 1933. It was designed by Dr Paul Cret of Philadelphia and is cleverly built into the Wall with steps and a simple, but imposing, arch at the top. The memorial commemorates 'the achievements and comradeship of the US and Royal Navies during the First World War'.

CASTLES AND WALLS

It is probable that Gibraltar has more defensive fortifications than any other settlement in the world, so there is much to interest the visitor with an historic bent. The oldest of these is the **Moorish Castle**, which dates from 1333 and was built on the site of an earlier fortress which may have dated from Tarik's initial occupation of the area in AD711. Originally the castle's fortifications stretched right down the edge of the town to Casemates Square, but they were destroyed in the various sieges. The main part of the castle remaining is the **Tower of Homage**, the walls of which are pitted with the scars inflicted in numerous conflicts. The castle can be viewed from the road above, but below it is hemmed in by blocks of flats. Entry is not permitted at present, as the castle functions as Gibraltar's prison and the roof overlooks the exercise yard. There are plans, however, to open the tower as a museum to house the 'Gibraltar – a City Under Siege', exhibition. At the lower end of the castle walls is an ancient gatehouse and nearby is **Stanley's Tower**, originally built in AD1160, but renovated several times since. Its clock dates from 1845.

Below: *View of the keep of the old Moorish Castle, Gibraltar's oldest building.*

Both the Moors and the Spanish built defensive walls along the western side of the Rock. The British strengthened the wall, now known as **Line Wall**, and extended it from Casemates to Rosia Bay. It was restructured and faced with Portland stone, the local limestone being too brittle.

See Map A–C4 | ★

DOLPHIN SAFARIS

Dolphin-watching has become increasingly popular in recent years and Gibraltar is one of the best places in Europe for this enjoyable pastime. Dolphins are aquatic mammals, members of the toothed whales found in seas all over the world (with a few

Above: *Dolphin Safaris have become a popular tourist attraction in recent years.*

similar in appearance being freshwater forms in some of the larger rivers of South America and Asia). Dolphins grow up to about 3–4.5m (10–15ft) long and have a short beak-like snout containing many sharp teeth with which they catch mainly fish. They travel in schools and when moving swiftly frequently leap from the water. One young dolphin is born at a time and carefully tended by the mother. They are common in the Straits of Gibraltar and will often travel alongside boats giving excellent viewing opportunities. Three varieties are frequently seen. The common dolphin (*Delphinus delphis*) grows to around 2m, with a streamlined body and a clearly defined beak. It is predominantly grey, but may have pale flanks. In open water it is usually seen in schools, often within sight of the shore. The bottle-nosed dolphin (*Turstops truncates*) is similar in appearance, but larger (up to 4m) and almost uniformly grey in colour. Striped dolphins are also occasionally seen. In addition to dolphins, various types of whales are often seen, such as the fin, sperm, pilot and orca. (In the early 20th century there was a thriving whaling station in Algeciras Bay). Sea turtles and flying fish are also sometimes seen.

Dolphin Safaris Dolphin World, ✉ Ferry Terminal, Water-port, ☎ 200 81000 No dolphins – money returned! Excellent commentary about the history of the Rock. No excursions Jan–Feb.

The Original Dolphin Safari, ✉ Marina Bay, ☎ 00 350 2007 1915, 🖥 www.dolphinsafari.gi Five trips a day in the summer. Has been running for over 30 years. (Don't confuse this company with another of the same name in La Linea.) No excursions Dec–Mar incl.

Dolphin Adventure, ✉ Marina Bay, ☎ 200 50650. New catamaran, environmental approach.

The Upper Rock Nature Reserve
⊠ Upper Rock
🕘 Open daily
09:30–19:00
🛎 Admission charge to Nature reserve and attractions for pedestrians and vehicles, with concessions. Reduced charge for nature reserve only. No credit cards.

Gibraltar Ornithological and Natural History Society (GONHS)
🖥 www.gibnet/gonhs

See Map D–G4 | ★

THE UPPER ROCK NATURE RESERVE

The name is something of a misnomer. As well as including areas of bare limestone, typical Mediterranean scrub and trees, the Upper Rock contains a number of popular sites, such as St Michael's Caves, the Great Siege Tunnels and the Apes' Den. These and other sites are usually visited by road and to get off the beaten track to observe the birds, flowers and other wildlife is difficult. Don't expect to see bird hides, marked trails and information boards. There is a move to refer to the area as the Upper Rock Nature Reserve and Heritage Site, which is much more acceptable. However you visit the Upper Rock, you have to pay for the privilege. All roads lead to the kiosk at Jews' Gate. A ticket will gain you entry to the main attractions, but if you just wish to walk around and peer over walls to look at flowers and birds, then a reduced-price ticket is available. Be prepared to be inconvenienced by taxis and minibuses and their occupants, particularly if

Below: *The Douglas footpath in the Upper Rock Nature Reserve is a haven from the tourists and the taxis.*

a cruise ship is in town. At Jews' Gate there is a viewing platform giving superb vistas over the Bay of Gibraltar and away south towards North Africa. Birds of the Upper Rock include blue rock thrush, scops owl, and Barbary partridge. There is a good range of wild flowers, exotic butterflies, lizards and, of course, the Barbary apes. The **Gibraltar Ornithological and Natural History Society** (GONHNS) is very active on the Rock and mans the observation point at Jews' Gate, where it records the passage of raptors.

See Map F–C4 | ★

ALAMEDA WILDLIFE PARK

The Alameda Wildlife Park is located in a corner of Gibraltar's Botanical Gardens on what was the old pitch and putt course. It can be approached either through the gardens or from Europa Road opposite the casino. The wildlife park dates from 1994, when birds and animals from a large container ship were impounded as they were being smuggled illegally into Europe. A home had to be found for the animals, so the wildlife park was set up. A team of volunteers from the Gibraltar Ornithological and Natural History Society were given funds to construct aviaries and enclosures. Birds and animals continue to arrive from customs seizures and other sources, so that the park grows by the year. Today, there are three permanent staff and a host of volunteers to run the park. The modest entrance fee is used to cover general maintenance, food bills and veterinarian expenses. Children will love the wildlife park, as many of the animals are those that make good household pets, such as the chipmunks and parrots. Especially popular are the pot-bellied pigs, the iguanas, the noisy peacocks and the snapping turtles. Of course, a wildlife park in Gibraltar would not be complete without a Barbary ape and the star of the park is Doris, an ape who had to be separated from her troop because she did not get on with the alpha female. Also of interest are the pair of ravens, with which it is hoped to breed. Any young will be released on the Rock, where it is hoped they will keep down gull numbers by taking their eggs.

Above: *The pot-bellied pig is among a number of fascinating animals at the Alameda Wildlife Park.*

Alameda Wildlife Park
⊠ Gibraltar Botanic Gardens, Red Sand Road, Gibraltar
☎ 200 72639
🖥 www.gibraltar.gi/alameda
🕐 Open winter 10:00–16:00, summer 10:00–18:00
💰 Small entrance fee (euros accepted), with concessions. Children under 5 enter free.

SIGHTSEEING

Above: *The Catholic Cathedral of St Mary the Crowned, built on the site of a Moorish mosque.*
Opposite*: St Andrew's Church of Scotland was built for the use of expats and servicemen.*

Places of Worship
Catholic Cathedral of St Mary the Crowned

The main Catholic church of Gibraltar was built on the site of a Moorish mosque. When the Spanish drove the Moors out of Gibraltar in 1462, the mosque was used as a Christian church. Later, the Catholic monarchs, Ferdinand and Isabella, decreed it should be stripped of its Moorish features and rebuilt in a Christian style. Ferdinand himself provided the money for the tower to be built. You can still see the mon-archs' coat of arms in the small courtyard. As with many mosques, the courtyard was once large and filled with orange trees and surrounded by cloisters, extending to the opposite side of what is now the Main Street. During the Great Siege the church was extensively damaged and a major rebuilding programme was necessary. The result was that the church was reduced in size, because Main Street needed to be straightened. The interior of the church is dominated by the high altar, which is along the lines of that in St Peters in Rome. Note, the beautiful marble columns. There are six other smaller Roman Catholic churches in Gibraltar.

✉ *Main Street*
🕐 *Services: Sunday Mass at 09:00, 10:30, 12:00 and 19:15.*

The Cathedral of the Holy Trinity

The Anglican cathedral dates back to the

early 19th century and was built in Classical style with prominent Moorish arches, both inside and on the exterior. Before its consecration it was used as an emergency hospital during the yellow fever epidemic in 1828. It was eventually consecrated 10 years later in the presence of the Dowager Queen Adelaide, the widow of William IV. Among the famous people buried here is General Sir George Don, perhaps the best known of Gibraltar's many Governors.

⊠ *Cathedral Square*
⊕ *Sunday services: 08:00, 10:30.*

St Andrew's Church of Scotland

This beautiful little Presbyterian church can be found in Governor's Parade. It was built to cater for expatriates and servicemen.

⊠ *Governor's Parade*
⊕ *Sunday worship: 10:30*
♿ *no admission fee*

The Great Synagogue

Gibraltar has a considerable Jewish community and their Great Synagogue has the distinction of being the oldest on the Iberian Peninsula, dating back to 1742. Located in Engineer Lane, it has been badly damaged twice, once by floods and later during the Great Siege. Its reconstruction is embellished by a striking bell gable, while the courtyard has a palm tree reputed to be over 200 years old. Guided tours of the Great Synagogue can be arranged. The town has three other smaller

The Jewish Community

There are currently over 600 Jews living at Gibraltar and the Rock has four synagogues and its own Hebrew primary school. There is also a kosher restaurant under the supervision of the Rabbi. Jews came to Gibraltar soon after the British took over the Rock, arriving from Morocco, London and Amsterdam. They have always played a full part in life on the Rock, treading a careful line between a deep sense of Gibraltar identity and an adherence to Jewish traditional values. Their most famous son was Sir Joshua Hassan, who dominated Gibraltar's political life for over 30 years in his capacity as the city's mayor and then as its Chief Minister.

Below: *A spectacular landmark on the southern tip of the Rock, the Ibrahim-Al-Ibrahim Mosque.*

synagogues.

✉ *Engineer's Lane*
☎ 200 76477

Ibrahim-Al-Ibrahim Mosque

To be found at Europa Point, *see page 20.*
✉ *Europa Point*
☎ 200 47694
🕐 *Phone for permission to visit.*

Historic Gates

There are a number of gates through the ancient walls of Gibraltar, some going back to the 14th century. Casemates Square, which is located on the site of the old Spanish town, can be entered via several gates. There are three **Casemates Gates**, the first of which was opened in 1727. The others followed in 1859 and 1884. Also providing access to Casemates Square is the **Landport Gate**. This was reconstructed by the British in 1729, on the site of earlier Moorish and Spanish gates. At one time it was the only landward access into the city. Its drawbridge was recently repaired and is in full working order. It was through this gate that British troops carried out a surprise sortie against the Spanish lines during the Great Siege. The **Ragged Staff Gates** are near

the main entrance to the dockyard. The first of the gates was opened for foot passage in 1843. There is much controversy about the origin of their name, the most popular theory linking it to the crest of Charles V, although it may refer to the rough nature of the stonework. There are further gates higher up in Charles V Wall. **Prince Edward's Gate**, dating from 1790, overlooks the Trafalgar Cemetery and is named after Queen Victoria's father, the Duke of Kent, who was Governor of Gibraltar from 1802 to 1803. The **Southport Gates** are a series of gates, the oldest of which dates from 1552 and is probably on the site of Tarik's original fortifications. The first gate is now for pedestrians and it bears the Spanish royal arms. The second gate, which is used for traffic, bears the arms of Queen Victoria and General Sir John Adye, a former Governor. This gate dates from 1883. The third, which is the widest of the gates, is the **Referendum Gate**. It was opened in 1967 and commemorates the Referendum when Gibraltarians voted overwhelmingly to retain their ties with Britain.

Museums and Galleries

Gibraltar's main museum is in **Bomb House Lane** (*see* page 28). There are also smaller museums at some other military sites, such as that at the **100-ton gun** (*see* page 25). Gibraltar's main art gallery is on the ground floor at the **John Mackintosh Hall**. Exhibitions change regularly and generally feature talented local artists. There is also an **Arts Centre** at ⊠ Prince Edward's Road, ⊕ 17:00–21:00 weekdays

A Wedding Location
The trend for weddings in exotic locations has not been lost on the authorities in Gibraltar, which has become a popular venue for stars and celebrities. John Lennon married Yoko Ono here. Other celebrities using Gibraltar include Roger Moore and the author Frederick Forsyth, while Sean Connery liked it so much that he married on the Rock twice! A couple can be married with a special licence within 24 hours of arriving in Gibraltar, providing that they satisfy legal requirements. Weddings can be held in a place of worship, in the Public Registrar's Office or in some of the top hotels. Two novel locations are the Dell in the Botanical Gardens and the cable car station at the top of the Rock. A number of organizations can provide the whole package, including the special licence, the wedding ceremony, photographs and even a beauty treatment for the bride. ⬛ www.gibraltar.gov.uk gives full information for anyone wishing to tie the knot on the Rock.

SIGHTSEEING

Above: *The Alameda Gardens, now known as the Botanical Gardens, display a range of Mediterranean plants.*

Hindu Community

Around six hundred Indians of Hindu origin currently live in Gibraltar. The majority came to the Rock as traders and today some 70% of the shops and bazaars in Main Street are run by Indians, specializing in electrical goods and textiles. In recent years Indians have diversified into other occupations and professions. They now have their own temple in Gibraltar and Hindu children attend mainstream schools. The current speaker of the House of Assembly is a Hindu.

---

only. Don't miss **The Gallery** in Casemates Square. This is the home of the **Gibraltar Fine Arts Association**, which holds regular exhibitions, promoting local artists. Paintings are imaginatively displayed in a series of vaults. All works are for sale.

Parks and Gardens
The Convent Gardens

The Convent Gardens of the Governor's residence are not normally open to the public, but there are occasional 'open days'. Take advantage of these as the gardens have some interesting plants and rare species of trees.

Having the governor of Gibraltar plant a tree in the garden of his official residence to mark special occasions is a great local tradition and almost every tree in the garden has a plaque marking a royal visit or the lifting of a siege. A flame tree from 1704 is the oldest specimen, planted when Britain took Gibraltar from Spain.

ACTIVITIES
Sport and Recreation

Football, cricket, hockey and athletics take place at the Victoria Stadium Sports Centre at the northern end of the Rock near to the port. There are also indoor facilities here for badminton, basketball and volleyball; ☎ 200 76409. There is a cricket pitch at Europa Point and a football pitch on reclaimed land close to the airport. There is no room for a golf course on the Rock, but there are over 30 courses on the neighbouring Costa del Sol – enough to satisfy any enthusiast. The Bay of Gibraltar is perfect for sailing (although the Straits, with their strong winds and tides, are a different matter). Sailing instruction is available at the marinas, where dinghies may be hired and tuition received. There is a string of marinas along the Costa del Sol, making cruising easy. Berths are often available on yachts heading for the Canary Islands or across the Atlantic. There are also opportunities for waterskiing. With over 30 wrecks, reefs and pinnacles, Gibraltar is amongst the best diving sites in the Mediterranean. A number of firms offer a complete diving service and provide courses for international qualifications. Visibility is usually near the 10m mark, but the water is colder than the rest of the Mediterranean, so a full wet suit is needed all the year round. The best dive sites are shown on Map D. Fishing is popular in the waters around Gibraltar both from boats and from shore locations such as moles and beaches, while deep-sea fishermen frequently catch tuna, sharks, swordfish and marlin.

Sailing
Alfer Sea School,
✉ Suite 5, International House, Bell Lane, PO Box 178, Gibraltar
☎ 200 79604
Gibraltar Sailing Centre, ✉ Queensway Quay Marina, Ragged Staff Wharf, Gibraltar
☎ 200 78554

Diving
Rock Marine, ✉ 7 The Square, Marina Bay, Gibraltar, ☎ 200 73147
Dive Charters PADI, ✉ 4 Admiral's Walk, Marina Bay, Gibraltar
☎ 200 45649

Fishing
Jalex Angling, ✉ Watergardens Quay, Waterport Wharf Road, Gibraltar, ☎ 200 70393
Fortuna Sport Fishing, ✉ Watergardens Quay, Gibraltar
☎ 956 173537

Below: Gibraltar has three excellent marinas that provide a full range of services for yachtsmen.

Above: *The Union Jack Steps celebrate the 1967 Referendum result to maintain ties with Britain.*

Boats may be hired for offshore fishing. Jun through to Nov is reckoned to be the top season.

Alternative Gibraltar
The Union Jack Steps

In 1967, a Referendum was held to decide whether Gibraltar should have closer ties with Spain or remain under the sovereignty of Britain. There was an overwhelming vote in favour of staying with Britain (12,138 to 44). To celebrate this event, the steps in an alleyway on the upper part of the Rock were painted in the colours of the Union Jack. Taxi drivers will point this out on the official tour.

Luis Photo Studio

This shop, at ⊠ 329C Main Street, must rank as the strangest retail outlet in Gibraltar. It holds a vast collection of photographs of just about all the ships and planes that have visited Gibraltar. Mention a ship that you might have served on and you will be asked which year this was. The computer clicks away and a photograph soon appears. This shop is, understandably, highly popular with ex-servicemen and women who visited or were stationed in Gibraltar; ☎/🖂 200 50710.

Police Force

The Royal Gibraltar Police Force is the second oldest police force in the world, being formed just nine months after Sir Robert Peel set up London's Metropolitan Police in 1829. There has always been close cooperation between Gibraltar's police and the military authorities. They are normally unarmed, apart from their truncheons, which replaced night sticks in 1894.

FUN FOR CHILDREN

Soldiers in the Wall

Near to Southport Gate is a glass-covered recess in the stone wall. Inside is a figure of a sentry. An inscription reads: 'A sentry of the KOSB, who reinforced the garrison in 1782 during the Great Siege'. On the other side of the road, but partly hidden by bushes, is a similar sentry box, with a life-sized model of a member of the 28th Gloucester Regiment, posted here from Menorca in November 1778.

The Tax Office Wall

Few people would want to have a close investigation of a tax office building, but spare a few moments to look at Gibraltar's tax office in the Main Street near Southport Gate. Embedded in the wall is a well-eroded ancient doorway. It is believed to have been brought from the parish church of Villa Vieja, in the oldest part of the town, which was badly damaged in the siege of 1727, and later demolished to make Casemates Square.

Fun for Children

Parents wanting to entertain their children will have to work hard in Gibraltar. There are, nevertheless, one or two possibilities. Youngsters with a love of nature will cer-

---

Tennis on The Costa del Sol

If tennis is your thing, hop on over to neighbouring Costa del Sol for a game or two at one of its smart tennis clubs or hotel tennis courts. Of the more than twenty clubs along the coast, the largest are at **Club Internacional de Tenis** (San Pedro), **Club Hotel Los Monteros** (Marbella), **Hotel Atalaya Park** in Estepona, **Hotel Don Carlos** (Marbella), and the **Puente Romano Hotel**, also in Marbella. Pick up a copy of the *Tennis on the Costa del Sol* brochure from the Spanish Tourist Board for more details.

Below: *The Luis Photo Studio in Main Street, which can provide a photograph of any ship or plane that has ever visited Gibraltar.*

Arranging your Dolphin Safari
There are as many as six firms running dolphin safaris from Gibraltar, plus others from La Linea. Tours usually last from one and a half to two hours, and money is often returned if dolphins are not sighted (a rare occurrence). Most of the tours are in comfortable boats, with outside or inside options, bars, toilets, and in one case underwater viewing. Some of the trips give an initial view of the Rock from the sea with an informative commentary. During the summer months, most organizations offer two or more trips a day and it is best to book ahead. In winter, it is best to phone in advance for details of sailings.

tainly enjoy the Barbary apes (*see* page 12) and will also find much of interest in the Alameda Wildlife Park in the Botanical Gardens (*see* page 35). Providing that they are not prone to seasickness, children will also like a **Dolphin Safari** (*see* page 33). Several companies run trips from the marinas. For a bucket and spade holiday, go no further than the beach at Catalan Bay. There is little or no sand at Camp Bay, but a series of seawater swimming pools with slides will attract children. There are many more possibilities if parents are prepared to go further afield, particularly along the Costa del Sol. Six kilometres (3.7 miles) east of Estepona is the excellent **Selwo Safari Park**, complete with lions, tigers, bears, a huge walkthrough aviary and truck rides along wild west scenery. ☎ 902 190402, 🖳 www.selwo.es ⊙ 10:00–18:00 Oct–May, 10:00–20:00 Jun–Sep, closed for parts of Nov, Dec, Jan and Feb, 🔔 the entrance fee is pricey.

Further east there are two aquaparks, one at Torremolinos and the other at Fuengirola (*see* page 75). A major attraction, and the area's oldest and biggest amusement park, is **Tivoli World**. As well as exciting rides and slides, there are folk and pop shows, musicals and children's events, plus a range of eating outlets. Tivoli World is located at Arroyo de la Miel, near Benálmadena, ☎ 952 577016, 🖳 www.tivolicostadelsol.com ⊙ 11:00–21:00 Jan–Mar; 16:00–01:00 Apr–May and mid-Sep to Oct; 17:00–02:00 Jun to early Sep; 18:00–02:30 Jul–Aug; 11:00–21:00 Sun, Nov and Dec; open weekends only during winter. Rides are extra to the admission price. Also at Benálmadena, in the marina, is **Sea Life**, a marine aquarium with what is probably Europe's largest shark collection. ☎ 952 560150, ⌨ www. sealife.es ⊕ 10:00–20:00 Jun, 10:00–midnight Jul and Aug, 10:00–18:00 Sep–May.

Walking Tour

It is possible to walk from the Main Street to the top of the Rock, with a number of options en route. Good footwear is essential and, in the summer, some sun screen is advisable. Start by locating the **Garrison Library** opposite the Elliot Hotel. Climb the steps along the side of the library and keep walking uphill until you reach a star-shaped road junction. Here you will see to the right the **Union Jack Steps** that date from the 1967 Referendum. Climb up the steps until it becomes a rough track. After 100m (109yd) you will find on the left some steps with metal railings. At the top of the steps, turn left and walk along the road uphill to **Devil's Gap Battery**. The Battery dates from the late 1800s and although it is in a derelict state, it still retains the two 152.4 cm (6in) coastal defence guns that saw action in World War II. This makes a good photo stop. After leaving Devil's Gap Battery the road turns sharply to the south at which point walkers should continue uphill in that direction for around 400m (438yd), passing under the **Cable Car** cables and arriving at the **Apes' Den**. This area is a popular stopping place for tourists taking the taxi tour and is often very busy. Instead of taking the roads to the top of the Rock (and paying the entrance fee at Jews' Gate), climb up the steps of the zigzag **King Charles V Wall**. Care should be taken as the

Above: *The Apes' Den is a popular stop on the way to the summit of the Rock.*

O'Hara's Battery
These gun emplacements were constructed between 1888 and 1890 and named after General Charles O'Hara, Governor of Gibraltar 1787–91. They replaced a round observation tower, which stood on what was known as Sugar Loaf Hill. The battery has had a variety of armaments over the years and was fully mobilized during World War I, when its nine-inch guns, which had a range of 16 miles, engaged with enemy submarines. It was also manned during World War II when it sustained some damage during air raids.

Above: *The Mediterranean steps from O'Hara's Battery. This is a good place to spot the Barbary partridge.*

Steps are in a bad state of repair; they are effectively out-of-bounds, but many walkers still use them on a daily basis. The steps lead to the summit ridge and it was close to this point that 500 Spanish soldiers scaled the east face of the Rock in 1704 helped by a shepherd along an old goat track. They had made their way from Catalan Bay a thousand feet below with the intention of overthrowing the garrison, but they were discovered and taken prisoner. The path was destroyed soon afterwards. The summit path leads to an old **Moorish Lookout Tower**. Little is known about the history of the tower, but it is amazing that this simple structure has survived the ravages of time.

For an alternative walk to the summit, take a taxi or walk to **Jews' Gate**. Here you will need to pay an entrance fee to the Upper Rock. There is a viewing point nearby (*see* page 34) and also the Gibraltar Ornithological and Natural History Society's information kiosk. A pathway from here leads along an old cultivation terrace and through a small copse to the start of the **Mediterranean Steps**. The first part of the walk is easy, but the second, longer part is quite demanding, eventually reaching the big guns of **O'Hara's Battery**. This World War I gun emplacement provides spectacular views of the water catchments, the Costa del Sol and the coastline of North Africa. Anyone scared of heights should not attempt this vertiginous walk, but it is the best place on the Rock for observing flora and fauna. There is a good chance of seeing the Barbary partridge, which was probably introduced by British servicemen in the 19th century as a game bird. This is the only place on the mainland of Europe where it is found. This is also an excellent area for finding birds such as the blue rock thrush and the peregrine falcon, as well as observing the raptor migration in spring and autumn.

Organized Tours

Gibraltar taxi drivers provide an 'official tour of the Rock' by taxi or minibus for a minimum of four people. Tours leave from a variety of places, including the frontier, Casemates Square, the coach park, the cruise terminal and Trafalgar Cemetery. The tours visit the Upper Rock including Jews' Gate, St Michael's Caves, the Barbary apes, the Great Siege Tunnels and the Moorish Castle. Entry fees are included in the price of the tour. The taxi drivers provide a knowledgeable account of the social history and geography of the Rock.

There are numerous travel agents in Gibraltar. Bland Travel provide an historical tour of the Rock; additional to the taxi drivers' tour it also includes Catalan Bay. Other agents offering Rock tours include Exchange Travel and Parodytur. All three companies provide day trips to Tangier, usually via Tarifa and the fast catamaran. Bland also offers a longer trip to

---

Gibraltar's Main Travel Agents

Bland Travel
✉ Cloister Building, Gibraltar
☎ 200 77221
📠 200 79244

Exchange Travel
✉ 241 Main Street, Gibraltar
☎ 200 76151
📠 200 40936

Parodytur
✉ 6 Cathedral Square, Gibraltar
☎ 200 76070
📠 200 40054

Below: *St Michael's lower caves can only be accessed on an organized tour.*

Car and Cycle Hire

Avis
✉ Bayside Road, Gibraltar
☎ 956 795507

Hertz
✉ 13 Winston Churchill Avenue, Gibraltar
☎ 200 42737

Budget
✉ Regal House, Gibraltar
☎ 200 79666

Niza Cars
✉ Air Terminal, Gibraltar
☎ 956 757537

Rentabike
✉ 36b Waterport Circle, Sheppard's Marina
☎ 200 70420

Below: *A ferry transporting tour groups arrives at the port of Tangier.*

Tangier that includes a visit to Tetuan. Excursions to various parts of southern Spain are also provided by Bland, who visit Ronda, Jerez (with a visit to a sherry bodega and the famous Spanish Equestrian School) and the resorts of Marbella and Puerto Banús. Bland's weekend highlight is their Marmalade Run to Estepona and Casares, with a drive through the orange and lemon groves and a visit to a street market. A meal is included on some of the longer trips.

Car Hire

Self-drive cars are readily available for hire and can be used for trips into Spain. Rates vary, with international firms generally more expensive than local firms (although their back-up if things go wrong is usually better). Cars are generally delivered with a full tank of petrol and should be returned full. Hire is restricted to drivers between the ages of 23 and 70 and a driving licence should be held for at least three years. An International Driving Permit may be requested from non-EU visitors. Cycles can also be hired.

Left: *The Last Shop in Europe is located right on the southern tip of Gibraltar's Europa Point.*

SHOPPING
Arts & Crafts

Gibraltar is something of a shoppers' paradise, with the main attraction being duty-free goods. Cigarettes, for example, are half the cost of what they are in Spain and a third of the UK price. There are similar bargains to be had with alcohol, particularly spirits. Petrol is also cheap. It is little wonder that Spaniards and expatriates on the Costa del Sol hop over the border for their shopping. Gibraltar's shopping centre is **Main Street**, but it is worth exploring the side streets and alleys, especially **Irish Town** and **Engineer's Lane**. There are branches of some of the UK's shopping institutions and other European chain stores, such as **Marks and Spencer**, **BHS**, **Benetton**, **Top Shop Dorothy Perkins** and the **Body Shop**. The biggest supermarket is **Morrison's**, built on reclaimed land near the port. Indian-run bazaars have always been a feature of the Rock's shopping scene, specializing today in electronic goods, such as videos, computers and cameras, and home textiles. Other shops concentrate on perfumes and cosmetics, offering much cheaper prices than Spain and the UK. There are a number of long-established jewellers, specializing in gold, silver, diamonds and watches, generally undercutting their Spanish equivalents by around 35%. There are several of antique stores in Gibraltar, some dealing in items with military connections. Shops generally open at 10:00 and stay open until 19:00 on weekdays, but close at 13:30 on Saturdays Late-night shopping is on Thursdays. Just about everything closes on Sunday, apart from Morrison's the supermarket. Sales staff are generally bilingual in both English and Spanish. Remember that in some shops a little gentle haggling is tolerated, particularly with expensive items. Sterling, the Gibraltar pound, Euros and even US dollars can be used and all the main international credit cards are acceptable. With a little persuasion, change can be given in the currency of your choice.

Book Sellers
Gibraltar Bookshop

This is the Rock's best bookshop, selling a variety of novels, factual books about the Rock, and also magazines.

⊠ 300 Main Street,
☎ 200 71894

Cosmetics and Perfumes
S.M. Seruya

The place to visit for taking your duty-free perfume back over the border. Also jewellery and Lladró.

⊠ 2/6 Main Street,
☎ 200 73194

Star of India

A wide range of cosmetics available with helpful and expert staff.

⊠ 108 Main Street,
☎ 200 75792

Clothes and Fashion
Marks and Spencer

Spaniards and expats flock over the border to buy their clothes and other items at this well-known English institution.

⊠ 215 Main Street

Monsoon

A wide range of ladies' fashion items available at reasonable prices.

⊠ 215 Main Street,
☎ 200 70175

Marble Arc

An unusual range of both men's and women's fashions and accessories.

⊠ 255 Main Street,
☎ 200 76176

Computers and Electronics
Carlos

The ultimate in digital technology including cameras, computers and DVD players.

Gibraltar's Favourite Son

John Galliano, a.k.a. Juan Carlos Antonio Galliano-Guillen, one of the most flamboyant figures in the fashion world, was born in Gibraltar in 1960 to a Spanish mother and a Gibraltarian father. The family moved to Streatham in London when John was six. He graduated with honours from London's St Martin's School of Art and moved into the fashion world. He gained the British Designer of the Year Award on no fewer than four occasions, before he moved to Paris. He worked for Givenchy and later Christian Dior. In 1997, Galliano was honoured by the Gibraltar government, when a series of stamps featuring his designs were issued. In 2001 he was awarded the CBE by Her Majesty the Queen. His most recent visit to the Rock was in 2003, when he buried his father in the North Front Cemetery.

⊠ 89 Main Street,
☎ 200 78841

Newton Systems
Specialist Apple Mac
and PC service, as well
as software and
maintenance.
⊠ 41–43 Engineer's
Lane, ☎ 200 41312

Liberty Electronics
Specializes in home
electronics, computers
and car stereo systems.
⊠ 62–65 Main Street,
☎ 200 76912

Khubchands
Family-run firm with a
wide range of home
appliances and leisure
products.
⊠ 55 Main Street,
☎ 200 78382

Jewellery
Crown Jewels
HIgh-class jeweller on
the Main Street.
⊠ 105 Main Street,
☎ 200 77756

Jewels and Gems
Specialist in jewellery,
gold and silver and
gemstones.
⊠ 122 Main Street,
☎ 200 48841

Gache and Co. Ltd
This is an old, estab-
lished firm dealing
with jewellery, sports
trophies and optical
items.
⊠ 266 Main Street,
☎ 200 75757

Regency
Specialist in Swiss-
made jewellery and
watches.
⊠ 94 Main Street,
☎ 200 59904

Sakarta
Experts in the field of
South Sea and fresh-
water pearls.
⊠ 92 Main Street,
☎ 200 77240

Below: *The shops lining Gibraltar's Main Street offer a very satisfying retail experience, with shops selling everything from books and jewellery to designer fashion and exquisite blown-glass objects.*

More Markets

There are other markets accross the border in Spain. The one in **La Línea** is a small-scale affair, but there are several in **Algeciras**. The biggest is the daily market in Plaza Palma by the port, which is particularly lively on Saturday mornings. **Estepona** has a busy daily fish market and a covered market in Calle Castillo.

Blue Spirit

Gibraltar Arms keyrings, stylish watches and Italian jewellery.

✉ 221 Main Street, ☎ 200 74163

Mobile Phones
Kris

All your mobile phone requirements.

✉ 5 Casemates Square, ☎ 200 77197

Glassware
Gibraltar Glass and Crystal

Watch the glass blowers at work and then buy their exquisite products.

✉ Casemates Square, ☎ 200 50136

Duty-Free Alcohol and Tobacco
La Casa del Habano

Wines, spirits and Cuban cigars.

✉ 41 Main Street, ☎ 200 78666

Saccone and Speed

Wine, spirits and tobacco merchants.

✉ 35 Devil's Tower Road, ☎ 200 74600

Anglo Hispano

Ideally placed on Main Street for your duty-free wine, spirits and tobacco, before going back over the border.

✉ 55 Main Street, ☎ 200 77210

Markets

There are currently three markets in Gibraltar, all close together: The **Public Market** is an indoor market located just outside the Casemates Gate. It sells seafood, fruit, vegetables and meat. The **Old Fish Market** is next to the Public Market, and the **Gibraltar Street Market** is held on Wednesdays, Fridays and Saturdays from 09:00–18:00 just off Main Street near the Casemates roundabout; it sells household goods, clothing and second-hand books. There is also a small **flea market** at Marina Bay on Saturdays from 12:00–17:00.

WHERE TO STAY

A small place such as Gibraltar will obviously have a limited number of accommodation options, but in fact there is sufficient choice for most visitors, however, don't expect any hotels in the luxury range – even the Rock Hotel, with its old colonial atmosphere, does not match up to some of the beach hotels of the Costa del Sol or the *paradores* of inland Andalucía.

Nevertheless, most visitors will find some accommodation to suit them. Businessmen tend to stay in the town centre hotels such as the Bristol or the Elliott, while the Caleta, on the east side of the Rock, attracts those in search of a beach holiday or those on a wedding package. The youth hostel does good business, but then there is little else in the budget category, so that the *pensiones* in La Línea across the border become an attractive alternative. Hotels may be booked through the Gibraltar Tourist Office ☎ 200 75000, via travel firms such as Blands ☎ 200 77221, or directly with the hotels, who will be able to give details of any special offers. Information is given for other hotels along the excursion routes, in case overnight stops are required.

> **What's in a Name?**
> Many of the small towns of southwestern Andalucía, such as Vejer, Conil, Zahara and Arcos, have the place-name suffix 'de la Frontera' or 'of the frontier'. This goes back to the days when the land was being contested by the Christians and the Moors. Battles raged backwards and forwards and these towns for a time formed the boundary between the territories of the opposing forces.

Below: *Built in 1932 by the Marquis of Bute, the rooms of this colonial-style hotel overlook the sea, offering stunning views from the balconies.*

ACCOMMODATION

Gibraltar

• LUXURY
The Rock Hotel
(Map D–E4)

This historic hotel was built in 1932 by the Marquis of Bute and offers a standard of service reflecting a more genteel era. It has a superb hillside location overlooking the Bay of Gibraltar. Its 104 rooms have all facilities, including balcony and sea view. Pool open in summer. Good restaurant. Rooms with facilities for the disabled.
⊠ *Europa Road,* ☎ *200 73000,* 📠 *200 73513,* 🖳 *www.rockhotel gibraltar.com* 🖰 *rock hotel@gibtelecom.net*

• MID-RANGE
The O'Callaghan Eliott Hotel (Map C–E3)

Recently refurbished town centre hotel. Its rooftop pool has panoramic views of the Rock and North Africa. Gym, sauna and conference facilities. Fine restaurants, entertainment and piano bar.
⊠ *Governor's Parade,*
☎ *200 70500,* 📠 *200 70243,* 🖰 *eliott@ gibnet.gi* 🖳 *www. ocallaghanhotels.com*

The Caleta Hotel
(Map D–G5)

Occupies a magnificent position on a headland at the southern end of Catalan Bay on the east side of the Rock. Pool and nearby beach. Piano and cocktail bars and an Italian restaurant, which is one of the best in Gibraltar; 160 rooms.
⊠ *Sir Herbert Miles Rd, Catalan Bay,* ☎ *200 76501,* 📠 *200 71050,* 🖳 *www.caletahotel. com* 🖰 *sales@caleta hotel.gi and* 🖰 *reser vations@caletahotel.gi*

Bristol Hotel
(Map C–E4)

Gibraltar's oldest hotel, centrally located close to shops and restaurants. Pool. No evening meals; 60 rooms.
⊠ *10 Cathedral Square,* ☎ *200 76800,* 📠 *200 76613,* 🖳 *www. gibraltar.gi/bristol hotel* 🖰 *bristhtl@ gibnet.gi*

• BUDGET
Queens Hotel
(Map C–I3)

Budget hotel a 3-min walk from Main Street. 62 rooms, mostly air conditioned, with TV and phone. Discounted rate for students.
⊠ *Boyd Street,* ☎ *200 74000,* 📠 *200 40030,* 🖳 *www.queenshotel.gi* 🖰 *queenshotel @gibtelecom.net*

Continental Hotel
(Map C–A3)

Small hotel in the town centre. Price includes continental breakfast. 17 rooms with air conditioning and TV.
⊠ *1 Engineer's Lane,* ☎ *200 76900,* 📠 *200 41702* 🖰 *contiho@ gibnet.gi*

Cannon Hotel
(Map C–D4)

Small basic, but attractive establishment in the town centre. Pleasant rooms, some with shared bathrooms. Good value for money.
⊠ *9 Cannon Lane,* ☎ *200 51711,* 📠 *200 51789,* 🖳 *www.cannonhotel.gi* 🖰 *cannon@gibnet.gi*

Emile Youth Hostel

(Map C–A4)

Cheap option with 43 places in single to eight-person rooms. Communal showers. Continental breakfast. Not recommended for lone women travellers. ☎ and ✆ 200 51106, ✆ emilehostel@yahoo.com

• APARTMENTS

Governor's Inn Apartments

(Map C–D3)

Double-bedded apartments with fully equipped kitchenette and satellite TV. Minimum stay applied during busy periods. ✉ 36 Governor's Street ☎ 200 44227, ✆ gibc@gibraltar.gi

Jade Travel Apartments

Modern studios and one-bedroom apartments, with TV, washing machine, microwave and pool ✉ Ocean Heights, ☎ 956 170173, 🖥 www.trivago.co.uk ✆ info@gibraltarholidays.com

La Línea

• BUDGET

Budget travellers might prefer to stay on the Spanish side of the border and try one of La Línea's pensiones.

Hostal Carlos II

(Map A–C4)

Comfortable, new accommodation in the town centre. All rooms with baths or showers and satellite TV. Good tapas bars nearby. ✉ Calle Mendes Nuñez 12, La Línea, ☎ 956 761303

Hostal la Campana

(Map A–C4)

Comfortable hostel just off the Plaza de la Constitución. All rooms have fans and TV and the restaurant has a decent menu de la dia. ✉ Calle Carboneras 3, La Línea, ☎ 956 173059

Ronda

• LUXURY

Parador de Ronda

(Map E–A2)

Occupies the old town hall and is perched on the edge of the gorge. Has all the luxury associated with this state-run and subsidized chain. Stupendous views from most of the rooms. Pool and traditional restaurant. ✉ Plaza de España s/n, Ronda, ☎ 952 877500, 🖥 www.parador.es ✆ ronda@parador.es

• MID-RANGE

Hotel Polo

(Map E–B1)

Traditional town centre hotel with the benefit of parking; 33 elegant rooms with balconied windows. Attractive communal areas. Good restaurant. ✉ Calle Mariano Soubirón 8, Ronda, ☎ 952 872449, ✆ reservas@hotelpolo.net 🖥 www.hotelpolo.net

Hotel Montelirio

(Map A–C1)

A new hotel in a converted palacio, located in the old town on the edge of the gorge. Fabulous lounge with a Mudéjar ceiling ✉ Calle Tenorio 8, Ronda, ☎ 952 873855, 🖥 www.hotelmontelirio.com

Hotel En Frente Arte ((Map A–C1)

A combined hotel, art school and gallery; 11 rooms, one in a converted tower, all in striking, modern décor. Pool, sauna and flower-filled patio. Price includes breakfast, lunch and all drinks.
⊠ *Calle Real 40, Ronda,* ☎ *952 879088,* 🖳 *www.enfrente arte.com*

• BUDGET
Hotel San Francisco

(Map E–C1)
A recently refurbished hostal which is the best of the budget possibilities in Ronda. All rooms have TV, air conditioning, heating.
⊠ *Calle Maria Cabrera 18, Ronda,* ☎ *952 873 299*

Costa del Sol

As one of Europe's top holiday hotspots, the Costa del Sol has a vast range of accommodation possibilities, although, apart from in Málaga, the budget end of the range has a poor choice.

Marbella

• LUXURY
Hotel el Fuerte

(Map A–D2)
A large, 263-room hotel sandwiched between the town centre and the beach. Plenty of facilities and a flower-filled garden, with pool, giving access to the beach.
⊠ *Avenida El Fuerte s/n, Marbella,* ☎ *952 768400,* 🖳 *www.hotel-elfuerte.es*

Refugio de Juanar

(Map A–D2)
Twenty rooms. Formerly a hunting lodge and parador, now run as a management cooperative. Peaceful mountain location with ibex and eagles and good walking possibilities. Cosy fires in winter, tennis and pool.
⊠ *Sierra Blanca, Ojen,* ☎ *952 881000,* 🖳 *www.juanar.com*

Hostal del Pilar

(Map A–D2)
Unusual building dating back to 1635 when it accommodated pilgrims travelling from Madrid. British owned, it encourages modern travellers. Bar and roof terrace.
⊠ *Calle Mesoncillo 4, Marbella,* ☎ *952 829936,* 🖳 *www.marbella-scene.com*

Fuengirola

• LUXURY
Hotel las Piramides

(Map A–E2)
At the quieter end of the *paseo,* it has a restaurant, parking, pool, tennis and is convenient for the beach. Entertainment in the evenings; 320 rooms.
⊠ *Calle Miguel Márquez 43, Fuengirola,* ☎ *952 470600,* 🖳 *www.hotellaspiramides.com*

• MID-RANGE
Hotel Puerto

(Map A–E2)
Faces the beach and has a tenth-floor swimming pool. Rooms have sea views and balconies. Heavily used by tour parties.
⊠ *Paseo Maritimo 32, Fuengirola,* ☎ *952 664503,* 🖳 *www.hotel elpuerto.com*

Mijas
• *LUXURY*
Hotel Mijas
(Map A–E2)
Luxury hotel; facilities include horse riding, golf, tennis and hydromassage.
✉ *Urbanización Tamisa 2, Mijas,* ☎ *952 485800,* 🖥 *www. hoteltrhmijas.com*

Torremolinos
• *LUXURY*
Hotel Tarik
(Map A–F2)
Huge Andalucían-style hotel located right on the seafront. Pool, gardens and attractive communal areas.
✉ *Paseo Maritimo 49, Torremolinos,* ☎ *952 382300,* 🖥 *www. hoteltarik.com*

Málaga
• *LUXURY*
Parador de Málaga-Gibralfaro
(Map F–C2)
A hilltop *parador* with wonderful views over the city and harbour. Rooftop pool. Restaurant with typical Andalucían gastronomy. Most rooms with terraces.
✉ *Camino de Gibralfaro s/n,* ☎ *952 221902,* 🖥 *www. parador.es*

AC Málaga Palacio
(Map F–B2)
Probably the best of the city's luxury options. Modern design and excellent facilities, including gym and pool. Stunning views over the seafront.
✉ *Avenida Cortina del Muelle 1, Málaga,* ☎ *952 220698,* 🖥 *www.achoteles.com*

• *MID-RANGE*
Hotel Don Curro
(Map A–F1)
Centrally located hotel favoured by businessmen. Comfortable, spacious

Below: *Hotels line the beach at Torremolinos on the Costa del Sol. Once a favourite haunt of the hippy crowd, it now caters for families.*

rooms. Bar and restaurant.
✉ *Calle Sancha de Lara 9, Málaga,* ☎ *952 227200,* 🖥 *www.hoteldoncurro.com*

Los Naranjos
(Map F–C2)
An attractive hotel located near the city's best beach and seafood restaurants. Typical Andalucían décor in the 41 rooms and public areas. Restaurant/bar serves tapas.
✉ *Calle Paseo de Sancha 35, Málaga,* ☎ *952 224316,* 🖥 *www.hotel-losnaranjos.com*

• BUDGET
Hostal Derby
(Map F–B2)
Cheap and cheerful hostel near the port. On the 4th floor of a building that looks like an office block. No credit cards.
✉ *Calle San Juan de Dios 1, Málaga,* ☎ *952 221301*

Hostal Avenidaz
(Map A–F1)
Centrally placed right on the Alameda; 25 clean rooms, some with a bath.
✉ *Avenida Principal 5, Málaga,* ☎ *952 217728*

Costa de la Luz
With fewer towns and resorts to the west of Gibraltar, there are fewer accommodation possibilities than on the Costa del Sol, but as the area is less popular, anyone looking for an overnight bed should find what they want, except, of course, in the height of the holiday season.

Tarifa
Keen windsurfers will find that there is accommodation here to suit most pockets.

• MID-RANGE
Dos Mares
(Map A–B4)
A series of cabins and bungalows, highly popular with families. Close to the beach, it has its own windsurfing and kite-surfing school, as well as stables.
✉ *Ctra. N340 km 79,* ☎ *956 684034,* 🖥 *www.dosmareshotel.com*

Hurricane Hotel
(Map A–B4)
Moroccan-style hotel set in subtropical gardens, with two pools and a restaurant. Home of the well-known Club Mistral windsurfing school and the Club Hipica horse-riding establishment.
✉ *Ctra. Cádiz,* ☎ *956 684919*

• BUDGET
Hostal Africa
(Map A–B4)
Restored townhouse in the middle of town, popular with backpackers.
✉ *Calle María Antonia Toledo 12,* ☎ *956 680220.*

Zahara de los Atunes
• MID-RANGE
Hotel Gran Sol
(Map B)
On a wide windy beach used by the

tuna fishermen. Comfortable hotel with pool and restaurant.
⊠ Avenida de la Playa 20, Zahara de los Atunes, ☎ 956 430309, 🖵 www.gransolhotel.com

Vejer de la Frontera
• *MID-RANGE*
Hotel Convento de San Francisco
(Map B)
Unique accommodation in a restored 17th-century monastery, with 25 austere but atmospheric rooms. Good restaurant in the former refectory.
⊠ Calle la Plazuela, Vejer de la Frontera.

Conil de la Frontera
• *MID-RANGE*
Flamenco
(Map B)
Cliff-top hotel, with 120 rooms all with air conditioning and wheelchair access. Closed January to February.
⊠ Calle Fuente de Gallo s/n, Conil

de la Frontera,
☎ 956 440711

• *BUDGET*
Tres Jotas
Comfortable 39-room pension on the main road into town. Has garage.
⊠ Calle San Sebastián 27, Conil de la Frontera,
☎ 956 440450

Cádiz
There is a wide range of accommodation in Cádiz to suit every taste and pocket.

• *LUXURY*
Atlantico Parador
(Map B)
The most upmarket hotel in the old town. Located at the point of the isthmus; 153 airconditioned rooms with great views over the Atlantic or the Bay of Cádiz. Pool and restaurant serving tasty seafood.
⊠ Avenida Duque de Nájera 9, Cádiz,
☎ 956 226905,
🖵 www.cadiz@parador.es

Playa Victoría
Modern beachfront hotel in the newer part of the city. Rooms with sea views and airconditioning
⊠ Plaza Glorieta Ingeniero La Cierva 4, Cádiz, ☎ 956 205100, 🖵 www.palafoxhoteles.com

• *MID-RANGE*
Hotel Francia y Paris
(Map B)
Attractive hotel in a charming square right in the heart of the old part of the city. Good option for exploring the sights.
⊠ Plaza San Francisco 6, Cádiz, ☎ 956 212319, 🖵 www.hotelfrancia.com

• *BUDGET*
Pensión Bahía
(Map B)
Probably the best cheap option in the old town. Just off the main plaza. All rooms have air conditioning, TV, bathroom and balcony.
⊠ Calle Plocia 5,
☎ 956 259061

Local dishes

It is difficult to define traditional Gibraltarian food – indeed there may be no such thing because of the multitude of influences brought by the Rock's diverse population. The food eaten in homes, however, is certainly different from that offered in restaurants and pubs, and, as yet, there is no definitive Gibraltarian restaurant in town. Perhaps the strongest influence on domestic cooking comes from Genoa in Italy, which has given us Gibraltar's national dish of calentita. It can be best described as a type of thick pancake made with chickpea flour, water, olive oil and salt and pepper. It is usually served with bread and butter.

EATING OUT

Visitors returning to Gibraltar after a gap of a number of years find that the biggest difference is the improvement in the standard and variety of food on offer. British food was once something of an international joke, typified by stodgy pastries and pies, greasy fish and chips with mushy peas and huge, unhealthy fry-ups for breakfast. In Gibraltar, this cuisine was perpetuated for years by the British troops stationed on the Rock. Today, the scene has changed. There are fewer servicemen based at Gibraltar and these have been replaced by day-trippers from the Spanish Costas and visitors from cruise liners and luxury yachts, who tend to demand more imaginative international food. Gibraltarians have been quick to respond and there are now a variety of cuisines and eateries available, with bistros, brasseries, wine bars and tapas bars, along with ethnic restaurants from India, China and other parts of the world.

Right: *A bustling lunchtime vibe at the Lord Nelson Café in Sandy Bay.*

What to Eat
The Traditional English Breakfast

Whilst tourists on the Costa del Sol may have to put up with a breakfast consisting of a roll, coffee and a fruit juice, in Gibraltar the 'traditional English breakfast' is alive and well. Indeed, in some establishments it may be served all

day. It usually consists of a fried egg, bacon, sausage and tomato, often supplemented by mushrooms, beans and black pudding. High-class establishments and top hotels may also offer kedgeree or kidneys. As a concession to the health-conscious, many of the items may now be grilled rather than fried. Whatever you choose, it's a meal that will set you up for a hard day's sightseeing.

Trends

The main axis for eating out in Gibraltar has shifted in recent years away from Main Street and down to the waterfront marinas. Restaurants such as Bianca's and Da Paulo at Marina Bay and Casa Pepe at Queensway Quay Marina serve international food with a Mediterranean slant. Meanwhile, some of Gibraltar's hotels have set up high-standard restaurants that are open to non-residents. Included in this category would be Nuno's at the Caleta Hotel, the Rib Room restaurant at the Rock Hotel and the Rooftop restaurant at the Elliot Hotel. In addition, many people are attracted to the simple beachside restaurants at Catalan Bay, where locally caught fresh seafood is always on offer.

Above: *Cafés, bistros and tapas bars line the walkways in the waterfront area.*

Liquid Gold

The Greek philosopher Homer described olive oil as 'liquid gold' and people have used this oil for over 6000 years. It was used as sacred oil, provided fuel for lamps and used to anoint athletes and embalm kings. Today olive oil is widely used in the Mediterranean countries as a cooking oil and olives as food. The fruit, which may be black or green, has the stone removed (pitted) and is often stuffed with pimento, cheese or almonds, forming a popular tapa dish. Remember, too, that olive oil is HEALTHY – it contributes to good complexions, efficient digestion and strong hearts. Moreover, olive oil contains no cholesterol.

Above: *Hearty English food at one of Gibraltar's many restaurants.*

Paella

Many of the restaurants in Gibraltar will offer the traditional Spanish dish of paella. In neighbouring Andalucía the paella will come in an iron pan and consist of rice coloured yellow with saffron, and a variety of seafood, including mussels, prawns and other shellfish. Further north, in Valencia province, meat, such as pork or chicken, replaces the seafood. On national holidays and festivals many of the beach bars and restaurants cook gigantic paellas two metres across to feed scores of people.

Fish and Chips

The traditional and succulent English fish and chips can be enjoyed in Gibraltar, making a filling meal at any time of the day or night. In Britain, cod and haddock are the usual fish and are deep-fried in batter, before being wrapped with the chips in newspaper to take away. Gibraltar puts its own slant on this meal, with the fish more likely to be sea bass or red mullet, while the chips will be cooked in olive oil rather than lard. For genuine fish and chips try Smith's in Main Street or Roy's in Convent Place.

What to Drink

As Gibraltar has no agricultural land, it does not grow its own grapes or produce any wine. Fortunately neighbouring Spain is one of the world's largest producers of wine and their bottles are readily available in supermarkets and restaurants, whose house wines are generally excellent. A refreshing drink in hot weather is *tinto de verano* (summer wine), which is cold red wine diluted with lemonade. Spanish spirits such as *coñac* (or brandy) and gin are of good quality. Most of Gibraltar's pubs concentrate on beer that they import from England, including some of the more widely available real ales. With high temperatures in the summer, many visitors prefer a cold lager-type beer, such as the Spanish favourites San Miguel and Cruz Campo. With no taxes, alcohol is cheap in Gibraltar, but many hotels and restaurants have a high mark-up on wine served at the table.

The English Pub

That typical feature of the English urban landscape, the 'public house', can also be experienced in Gibraltar. They were hugely popular with the British servicemen and women on the Rock and many pubs are still around today. But like their English counterparts, the pubs in Gibraltar have had to move with the times. Once purely drinking establishments, they are now obliged to offer food (some have separate dining rooms) and many feature live entertainment. Tables now spill out onto the pavement in typical Mediterranean style and English licensing hours are long gone. For an essential pub experience, try the Angry Friar in Main Street, the Clipper in Irish Town or the Horseshoe in Main Street.

Tapas

As an alternative to an evening meal in Gibraltar, why not slip over the border to La Linea and go on a tapas crawl? Tapas, or small snacks, are thought to have originated in Seville, where legend has it that drinkers protected their sherry from flies, dust and dripping ham with a cover or tapa, usually a slice of bread. Before long enterprising bartenders were putting food on the bread, and the rest, as they say, is history. Once free, tapas generally have to be paid for today. They were traditionally served cold, but many tapas are now popped into a microwave. Food varies enormously from simple olives and chunks of cheese or tortilla to some quite elaborate dishes. The traditional drink to accompany a tapa is fino sherry, but in reality anything goes.

Left: *A mind-boggling selection of whisky is on sale at this Gibraltar liquor store.*

Right: *Treat yourself to fine dining at The Rock Hotel's top-notch restaurant.*

Gibraltar
• *Luxury*
Bianca's

Popular restaurant on the quayside at Marina Bay with a large terrace. International food, with children's and vegetarian menus. Open 7 days a week, 09:00 till late. ✉ 6/7 Admiral's Walk, Marina Bay, ☎ 200 73379

Casa Pepe

Situated right on the waterfront at Queensway Quay. Serves a comprehensive and imaginative international menu. There is also a good range of tapas. ✉ 10 Queensway Quay Marina, ☎ 200 46967, ☺ Mon–Sat 11:00 till late

Claus on The Rock

Stylish restaurant serving a wide international cuisine. Noted for its fine wine and cigars. ✉ 14 Queensway Quay, ☎ 200 48686, ☻ lunch and dinner. Closed Sun.

La Mamela

Located at Catalan Bay close to a rock of the same name. Generally recognized as the best seafood restaurant in town, with succulent paellas and fish stews. ✉ Catalan Bay, ☎ 200 72373

Cheap Eating in Spain
While on an excursion from Gibraltar to Spain, a cheap way of having a lunch is to look for the *menu del dia* or menu of the day. Most restaurants will have this bargain option and it usually consists of a main course and a dessert, served with a roll and a drink such as a glass of wine, beer or a soft drink.

Café Solo

Italian restaurant in Casemates Square, specializing in pastas, pizzas and risottos, all prepared with flair.
⊠ Casemates Square, ☎ 200 44449

Da Paolo

International cuisine served on a water-front terrace. Also serves English break-fast and lunches.
⊠ Marina Bay, ☎ 200 76799, ⏰ 09:30 till late. Closed Sun.

Nuno's

High-class Italian restaurant at the Caleta Hotel. Terrace dining with wonder-ful views along the Spanish coast. Noted for its good wines and imaginative cooking.
⊠ Caleta Hotel, Sir Herbert Miles Road, ☎ 200 76501

The Rib Room

The Rock Hotel's top notch eatery, with a high standard of service and cuisine. Stunning views across the bay.

Resident pianist accompanies your meal. Comprehensive Sunday lunch.
⊠ The Rock Hotel, Europa Road, ☎ 200 73000, 🖳 www.rock hotelgibraltar.com ⏰ 19:00–22:00 daily.

Simon's Restaurant

Small intimate bistro in the town centre serving interesting ver-sions of old favourites.
⊠ 44 Cornwall's Lane, ☎ 200 47515, ⏰ Closed Sun.

Bunters

Long-established restaurant serving upmarket British dishes. Evenings only.
⊠ 1 College Lane, ☎ 200 70482, ⏰ Closed Sat.

Little Mermaid

Danish-owned restau-rant specializing in Scandinavian cuisine.
⊠ 4/5 Admiral's Walk, Marina Bay, ☎ 200 77660, ⏰ Closed Sun.

Thyme

Wine bar with bistro-style restaurant above.

International food from a menu that changes seasonally, with daily specials. Everything made on the premises from fresh ingredients.
⊠ 5 Cornwall's Lane, ☎ 200 49199, ⏰ 12:30–15:00 and 19:00 till late.

• BUDGET
Al Andaluz Bar Restaurant

Small town centre eatery serving a variety of food, including some Moroccan delicacies.
⏰ 08:00 till late.

Fancy That Sandwich Bar

Great place for rolls, sandwiches, pies and toasties.
⊠ Ground floor International Commercial Centre, ☎ 200 47262, ⏰ Mon–Fri 08:30–18:00, Sat 10:00–14:00.

Khan's Indian Cuisine

Eat in or takeaway. All the traditional Indian dishes.

Above: *A typical English-style pub is the Horseshoe in Main Street.*

⌧ *Unit 7–8, Watergardens,*
☎ *200 50015*

Piccadilly Garden Restaurant

Pleasant bar/restaurant close to the cable car station. Mixed Spanish/English food.
⌧ *3 Rosia Road,*
☎ *200 75758,*
⏲ *09:00 till late.*

The Real Taste of Cornwall

Pasties handmade in Cornwall and baked in Gibraltar with a variety of traditional and novel fillings.
⌧ *16 City Mill Lane,*
⏲ *10:00–late Mon–Sat.*

Pubs

All the traditional pubs in Gibraltar now serve food.

The Angry Friar

Typical British pub opposite the Convent. Large terrace with all-day food. Sunday roasts.
⌧ *278 Main Street,*
☎ *200 71570,*
⏲ *09:30 till midnight.*

The Clipper

Large popular bar serving home-made food. Sporting events on large screen.
⏲ *09:30 till midnight,*
⌧ *Irish Town,*
☎ *200 79791*

The Horseshoe

Town centre pub, always popular and busy. Typical English food plus curries.
⌧ *193 Main Street,*
☎ *200 77444,*
⏲ *09:00–late.*

The Royal Calpe

Traditional bar near the cathedral, serving pub food all day. Children's menu. Beer garden in rear.

✉ *176 Main Street,* ☎ *200 75890,* ⏰ *09:00 till midnight.*

Where to Eat on Excursions

Ronda

Don Miguel

If not the best food in Ronda, certainly the best view, with its terraces overlooking the bridge and gorge.

✉ *Plaza de España,* ☎ *952 871090*

Tragabuches

Named after a local torero and bandit, this restaurant is one of the best in Andalucía, serving modern dishes with flair and skill.

✉ *Calle José Aparicio 1,* ☎ *952 190291*

Relax

The only vegetarian restaurant in Ronda. Imaginative dishes cooked by the English owners. Restricted opening hours in winter.

✉ *Calle Los Remedios 27,* ☎ *952 877207*

There are a number of excellent tapas bars in Ronda. Try **Bar La Viña** at ✉ Calle Lorenzo Borrego Gómez 9, **Bodega La Verdad** at ✉ Calle Pedro Romero 3 or **La Leyenda** at ✉ Calle Los Remedios 7.

Marbella

There is an incredibly wide range of eating possibilities in Marbella to suit all tastes and pockets.

La Hacienda

Legendary restaurant founded by the Belgian chef, the late Paul Schiff. Nouveau cuisine of the highest order.

✉ *Urb. Las Chapas, N340 km 193,* ☎ *952 831267*

La Pesquera

Modestly priced seafood dishes under a thatched roof in a square just to the west of the old town.

✉ *Plaza de la Victoria,* ☎ *952 778054*

Fuengirola

Valparaiso

A restaurant popular with expats. Large dining terrace with superb views. Music and dancing most weekends.

✉ *Ctra. Fuengirola-Mijas km 4,* ☎ *952 485996*

For cheap but wholesome food, go to Fuengirola's pedestrianized **Calle Moncaya**, where there is a string of restaurants serving fresh seafood and bargain *menus del dia*.

Málaga

There are some superb restaurants and tapas bars in Málaga where you can enjoy traditional local specialities. As Málaga is not a tourist city the restaurants keep to Spanish eating hours. The seafront at Pedregalejo has some of the best seafood

---

Bolonia

Behind the beach at Bolonia there are a number of small restaurants which serve tasty, fresh seafood. These include:
Rios, Bolonia,
☎ 956 684 320.
Good fish menu with views over the ocean from its dining room.

---

restaurants and *chiringuitos* (beach bars) in Andalucía.

Antonio Martín

A celebrated fish restaurant on the Paseo Maritimo, often frequented by matadors from the nearby bullring.
✉ *Paseo Maritimo 4, Málaga,*
☎ *952 222113*

La Posada de Antonio

One of several restaurants that the actor Antonio Banderas (a Malagueño) has opened in the area. Traditional local specialities.
✉ *Plaza Mayor, Málaga,*
☎ *952 217069*

Tintero

A fascinating restaurant where waiters auction off dishes as they wander among the tables. Seafood specialities.
✉ *Playa del Dedo, El Palo, Málaga,*
☎ *952 204464*

Among the host of tapas bars, try **La Campana**, ✉ Calle Granada 35 near the cathedral; **Pitta Bar**, ✉ Calle Echegaray 8 close to the Picasso Museum and specializing in Moroccan-style tapas, and **Antigua Casa Guardia**, ✉ Alameda 18, said to be a favourite haunt of the youthful Picasso.

Costa de la Luz

An excursion from Gibraltar along the Atlantic coast of Spain will turn up some fine restaurants. Search out some of the simple *chiringuitos* (beach bars) that serve freshly caught seafood.

Below: *Paella is a typical Spanish dish of rice and seafood. The version from Valencia has meat instead of seafood.*

Tarifa

Souk

Moroccan ambience and African-inspired food. A useful experience for anyone about to take the ferry to North Africa.
✉ Calle Huerta del Rey 11, Tarifa,
☎ 956 627065

Mondrágora

Located behind the Church of San Mateo, this restaurant serves imaginative Moroccan food accompanied by North African music.
✉ Calle Independencia 3, Tarifa,
☎ 956 681291

Vejer de la Frontera

Mesón El Palenque

Economical option in a small square with outside seating. Meat and seafood tapas.
✉ Calle San Francisco 1,
☎ 956 641579

Conil de la Frontera

Restaurante la Fontanilla

Serves excellent seafood and succulent steaks from local cattle.
✉ Playa de la Fontanilla, Conil,
☎ 956 441130.
For fresh cheap seafood, try the two chiringuitos on the beach below the Hotel Fuerte Conil.

Cádiz

For the best eating experiences head for the large squares of Cádiz, which are surrounded by restaurants and tapas bars. The new town's beach has a number of heladerías, serving luscious ice creams and milk shakes. In addition, Cádiz has two of the best fish restaurants in Andalucía:

Achuri

Outstanding seafood and very popular with locals, so be prepared to book ahead.
✉ Calle Plocia 15, Cádiz,
☎ 956 221939

El Faro

Taberna-style restaurant producing some classy seafood including a renowned paella. Also produces some superb tapas. It is advisable to book ahead for a table at the restaurant.
✉ Calle San Felix 15, Cádiz, ☎ 956 211008

La Cigüena

Close to the main square. Dutch chef who specializes in game dishes.
✉ Calle Plocía 2, Cádiz,
☎ 956 250179

Arana

Stylish, modern restaurant alongside the main beach. Meat and seafood specialities.
✉ Paseo Maritimo 1, Cádiz,
☎ 956 205090

Cádiz abounds with atmospheric tapas bars. Try the following, many of which are in the Calle Zorilla area: **Mesón Cumbres Mayores**, **Cerveceria Aurelio** and **Gaditana**, none of which will disappoint.

ENTERTAINMENT

Although nobody would claim that Gibraltar is the entertainment capital of the western world, there is plenty to see and do in this tiny colony. Much of the evening activity centres on the pubs and restaurants, many of which feature live music. Although there are only two theatre venues, there is a great theatrical tradition on the Rock and the local media and the tourist office will have full details of performances. Gibraltar's hotels have lively cocktail bars and dance floors, and many visitors follow up this activity with a flutter at the casino.

Theatre and Music

Sadly, Gibraltar's beautiful Theatre Royal in Governor's Parade has been allowed to fall into disrepair and disuse, but there are plans to refurbish it. In the meantime, the only other purpose-built theatre is Ince's Hall at the south end of Main Street. There are also theatrical performances at the John Mackintosh Hall (part of the public library complex) in Main Street. There is also an open-air theatre in the

Botanical Gardens. There are around half a dozen amateur dramatic groups who put on plays, musicals, dance and light opera. Regrettably, there is no commercial cinema in Gibraltar.

Lighter Entertainment

For lighter evening entertainment, head for Gibraltar's pubs, bistros and wine bars, where there is often live music, karaoke, al fresco dancing and even the occasional flamenco show. At one end of the scale are the traditional English-style pubs, such as the Clipper and the Angry Friar, while on the other hand there are the cocktail bars of hotels such as The Rock and the Caleta, which have resident pianists and dance bands. Many of the restaurants, particularly those on the waterfront and the marinas, provide live music for diners and stay open until well after midnight.

Opposite: *Gibraltar on a moonlit night, seen from across the bay at La Línea.*
Below: *Gamble in style at the Stakis International Casino.*

Stakis International Casino

Gibraltar's casino is found on Europa Road, just past the Rock Hotel. There is no entrance fee and no membership or passport requirements. Punters can try Blackjack, American Roulette and Casino Stud, while there are also a vast number of slot machines. The luxurious surroundings include a first-class restaurant and some wonderful views. ⊠ 7 Europa Road, ☎ 200 76666.

Miss Gibraltar
A highlight of the social calendar is the annual election of Miss Gibraltar. Contestants are judged for beauty of face and figure, deportment, charm, poise, personality, intelligence and general conversation. Judging takes place in swimwear and evening dress and the event is often held in St Michael's Caves. The winner receives a cash prize of £3500 and entry to the Miss World competition. Visitors to the Rock should not bother to enter, as contestants have to be Gibraltarian (they should also be over 17, unmarried and not a mother).

Below: *A colourfully costumed flamenco dancer entertains onlookers with this passionate, traditional dance.*

Nightclubs, Bars and Discos

Gibraltar does not have much to offer in the way of nightclubs and discos. Most locals and tourists will make the trip to Costa del Sol if the urge to party through the night suddenly seizes them. Note that the nightlife on Costa del Sol gets underway after midnight on most evenings.

Torremolinos
With high-tech discos and glittering drag shows to lure the visitor, the variety of entertainment on offer is infinite in **Calle San Miguel**.

Benalmádena
Explore the slightly quieter area of **Arroyo de la Miel**, if too much neon and flash is not your scene.

Marbella
With its expensive clubs and fancy cocktail bars, Marbella's nightlife is definitely more upmarket than elsewhere on the Costa del Sol.

Puerto Banús
A great area to explore during the summer months, when the entire port is abuzz with people, partying and clubbing until dawn almost every night.

Flamenco
Originating from the gypsies of Seville, Jerez and Cádiz in the 19th century, flamenco is a passionate interweaving of music and dance that has become an integrated part of Spanish culture. For those who want to experience the real thing (as

FLAMENCO

Left: *The sunset turns Torremolinos on the Costa del Sol into a city of gold.*

opposed to the much-diluted, typical 'folk dancing' one sees in tourist resorts), ask at the tourist office in Gibraltar (⊠ Duke of Kent House, Cathedral Square, opposite the Anglican Cathedral, ☎ 200 45000, 🖳 www.gibraltar.gov.uk ⊕ 09:00–17:30 Mon–Fri). To find good flamenco on the Costa del Sol, it is best to join in with a *feria* in Málaga or Seville, where there are often performances by travelling artistes in backstreet *café cantates*. Dancers and musicians use flamenco to express great joy and agony, and there are varying levels of intensity: *grande* or *jondo* (deep); *intermedio*, which can sound somewhat oriental and is less profound; and *pequeno* or *canto chico*, which is lighter and much more joyful. Flamenco dances include the *sevillana*, *tango*, *farrucca*, *fandango* and *zambra* and note that not only is everything improvised – although the rhythms remain fixed, but instead of the dancer following the guitar, it is in fact the other way around, and when musician, dancer and onlookers (*afficionados*) attain that moment of understanding amongst each other, it is called *duende*.

Beware of Scooters
Owning a car in Gibraltar is a dubious privilege, owing to congestions and parking problems, so many citizens own scooters. These machines buzz around at great speed, often ignoring traffic signals, breaking the speed limits and making a mockery of the rules of the road. Visiting car drivers and pedestrians beware!

Public Holidays
New Year's Day • 1 January
Commonwealth Day • ca. 10 March
Good Friday • variable
Easter Monday • variable
May Day • variable during first week in May
Spring Bank Holiday • variable, last week in May
Queens Birthday • ca. 16 June
Gibraltar National Day • second week in September
Christmas Day • 25 December
Boxing Day • 26 December
Note that shops do not usually open on bank holidays.

EXCURSIONS

Gibraltar is ideally situated for forays into Spain and across to Morocco in North Africa. Though there are no train lines along the coast of Spain, there is a network of bus services from La Línea linking all the major towns. Cars may be hired cheaply in Gibraltar and can be insured for driving in Spain. This enables smaller off-the-beaten-track places to be visited. Note that in Spain, all museums should have free entry to citizens of EU countries.

The area to the east of Gibraltar is known as the **Costa del Sol** and stretches as far as the city of **Málaga**. This is the birthplace of Picasso and boasts an 11th-century castle, several excellent museums and a large cathedral. Málaga is famous for its traditional Easter week celebrations and its annual *Feria* or fair. A string of holiday resorts stretches westward. **Torremolinos**, once the haunt of hippies, is now cleaning up its act. **Fuengirola** and **Estepona** are typical family resorts, while **Marbella** attracts the rich and famous. Just inland are attractive hill villages, such as **Mijas** and **Casares**. There are numerous family attractions such as aquaparks, safari parks and aquariums, while for adults there is the highest concentration of golf courses on mainland Europe.

To the west of Gibraltar lies the **Costa de la Luz**, a totally different area to its eastern neighbour. Deserted windswept beaches are interspersed with small resorts, such as **Conil**, fishing ports like **Barbate**, and hill villages, the most impressive of which is **Vejer de la Frontera**. The ferry port of **Tarifa** is Europe's premier windsurfing location. Don't miss the Roman ruins of Baelo Claudio, near the village of **Bolonia**. At the northern end of the

Costa de la Luz is the city and port of **Cádiz**. Its narrow streets, squares and monuments make it an absolute gem. There is a clutch of excellent museums, a cathedral with an eye-catching gold dome and a theatre named after Manuel de Falla, the musician who was born in the city.

A favourite excursion is to the historic city of **Ronda**, high up on a limestone plateau and split in half by El Tajo, a gorge some 120m deep. The old part of the town has many Moorish remains including baths, a bridge and the rather haphazard street plan. Ronda is the home of bullfighting and claims to have the oldest bullring in Spain. There are several good museums, including one devoted to banditry.

While in Gibraltar, why not visit North Africa? **Morocco** can be clearly seen on most days across the Straits and is reached in a mere 35 minutes by fast catamaran from Tarifa. The most popular destination is **Tangier**. The usual day excursion offers a coach tour of the city, the chance to ride a camel, a walk around the souks and a traditional Moroccan meal.

The Costa del Sol

After crossing the border at La Línea (there is little to detain the tourist here), the coast road eastwards passes the hill village of **San Roque**, to which many Gibraltarians fled when the British took over the Rock. Shortly, the upper-crust resort area of **Sotogrande** is reached. It

Fuengirola
Distance from Gibraltar: 77km (49 miles)
Tourist Information
⊠ Avda Jesus Rien 6 (at the old railway station), ⏰ Mon–Fri 09:30–14:00 and 16:30–19:00; Sat 10:00–13:00.
⊠ Avda José Cela 6, ☎ 952 666301, ⏰ daily 10:00 until dusk, 💰 entrance fee.
Parque Aquático Mijas
⊠ Fuengirola by-pass, ☎ 952 460404, ⏰ May–Sep daily from 10:00, closure according to season.
Aquapark Torremolinos
⊠ Torremolinos by-pass, ☎ 952 388888, ⏰ May–Sept daily 10:00–18:00; Jul–Aug until 19:00.
Tivoli World
⊠ Arroyo de la Miel, Benalmádena, ☎ 952 441896, ⏰ daily 18:00–02:00, 🖥 www.tivolicostadelsol.com 💰 admission fee, under 5s free.

EXCURSIONS

Málaga
**Distance from
Gibraltar:** 106 km
(66 miles)
**Regional Tourist
Office**, ✉ Pasaje
Chinitas 4, ☎ 952
213446, ⊕ Mon–Fri
08:30–20:00 and
14:00–20:00, Sat and
Sun 10:00–14:00.
Municipal Office
✉ Avda de Cervantes
1, ☎ 952 134730, ⊕
Mon–Fri 08:00–14:30
and 16:00–19:00, Sat
and Sun 09:30–13:30.
**Alcazaba Museo
Archaeológico**
✉ Gibralfaro, ☎ 952
216005, ⊕ Tue–Sun
09:30–20:00, ♿ joint
entry price with
Gibralfaro Castle.
**Centro de Arte
Contemporaneo**
✉ Calle Alemania s/n,
☎ 952 120055,
⊕ Tue–Sun 10:00–
20:00, ♿ entry free.
**Museo de Artes y
Tradiciones Populares**
✉ Calle Pasillo Santa
Isabel 10, ⊕ Mon–Fri
10:00–13:00 and
16:00–19:00, Sat
10:00–13:30.

has many luxury properties, the Valderrama world-class golf course, a polo ground and a harbour full of pricey yachts and suitably expensive restaurants. A winding road leads inland for 18km to **Casares**, claimed to be the most photographed village in Spain. Its white-washed houses clothe the side of a hill, which is capped by a 13th-century Moorish fortress on Roman foundations. Casares is said to have derived its name from Julius Caesar, who may have been cured of his liver complaints by the sulphur springs at nearby Manilva.

The family resort of **Estepona** has a large marina and a superb sandy beach, but little else. There is ribbon development from here all the way to Málaga and beyond, with a string of beautifully manicured golf courses and a forest of building cranes indicating yet more luxury apartments.

Marbella is the top resort on the Costa del Sol and a social step above its neighbours to the east and west. Backed by a distinctive limestone mountain, it has a superb beach, historic old town, swish shops and fine restaurants, as well as the chance of spotting someone famous. The old town surrounds the attractive Plaza de los Naranjos. The old Moorish street plan remains, with plant-

filled atmospheric alley-ways and traces of the old city walls. There are a number of museums, including the Museo del Grabado Español Contemperáneo, showing contemporary Spanish prints, and the Museo del Bonsai, with its imaginatively displayed miniature trees.

Two miles west of Marbella is **Puerto Banús**, a marina development with floating gin palaces alongside gold Rolls Royces and tourists gaping at anyone who might be a celebrity. The area between Marbella and Puerto Banus is known as the 'Golden Mile' and is the home of Arab princes, arms dealers, media stars, famous sportsmen and more than one notorious criminal.

Fuengirola is a multi-purpose town. It is a family holiday resort, with a large fishing fleet and much light industry in its suburbs. The west of the town is dominated by Sohail Castle, which goes back to Roman times, but has been rebuilt on numerous occasions. There is plenty to interest children at Fuengirola and nearby, including an excellent little zoo, two aquaparks and the Tivoli World theme park.

Just 7km inland from Fuengirola is the stunning hill village of **Mijas**. Geared, these days, to catering for tourists, with donkey rides, English-run restaurants and garish souvenirs, Mijas nevertheless, has a certain charm and is well worth a visit. Its history goes back to the Moors, who built the defensive walls on top of steep cliffs. From here there is a panoramic walk giving fantastic views over the coastline and the pine-covered mountains.

Málaga, the largest town and administrative centre of the Costa del Sol, has much of interest. First impressions can be discouraging, as the city is ringed with industrial estates and apartment blocks. The central core, however, is graced by a majestic, if unfinished Gothic cathedral surrounded by sun-baked ochre buildings, narrow pedestri-

Above: *The marina at Puerto Banús is worth a visit, if only to see how the other half lives*
Opposite: *The Plaza de los Naranjos in Marbella is named after its many orange trees.*

<u>Málaga</u>
Museo Picasso
✉ Palacio de Buenavista, Calle San Agustin 8, ☎ 952 602731, 🖳 www.museopicasso malaga.org
🕓 Tue–Thu 10:00–20:00, Fri–Sat 10:00–21:00, Sun 10:00–20:00, 💰 entry fee.
La Concepción Botanical Gardens
✉ 4 km north of city centre, ☎ 952 252148, 🕓 daily 09:30–19:00, winter 10:00–17:30, 💰 entry fee.

Resisting The Time Share Touts

Visitors who cross the border to the Costa del Sol will be lucky if they are not pestered by time share touts. These are usually young people whose job it is to entice tourists to come along to a time-share sales office. The latest enticement is the scratch card and if you find you have won something (and you invariably have) it takes a strong will not to go along to collect it. The sales person then subjects the visitor to a lengthy presentation, which involves buying an apartment for life for a certain period each year, with the possibility of swapping your week for a similar booking elsewhere in the time-share world. For some people this has advantages, while for others it might be better to buy their own property. The best advice is to sum up the pros and cons and don't sign anything until you are sure that time-share is for you.

anized streets and more bars per square mile than any other town in Europe. Dominating the city is the ruined Gibralfaro Castle, built by the Moors in the early 14th century. Nearby is the Alcazaba, a fortress and palace built by the Moors but containing Phoenician and Roman masonry in the walls. The main palace building now houses the Archaeological Museum. There are plenty of other museums, including the Centro de Arte Contemporaneo, Malaga's answer to London's Tate Modern, and the Museo de Artes y Tradiciones Populares (a fascinating social history museum). The Museo Picasso is Malaga's latest and most prestigious museum and houses many of the artist's most famous works. Keen gardeners should head for the La Concepción Botanical Gardens on the outskirts of the city. Paths lead through a tamed jungle of palms, dragon trees, camellias, jacarandas and a Norfolk Island pine tree claimed to be the largest in Andalucía.

The Costa de la Luz

The 'Coast of Light' stretches from Algeciras to Cádiz in the north and is a totally different world to the Costa del Sol to the east. This is where the Spaniards take their holidays and the English language is rarely heard. Leaving Gibraltar and La Línea behind, the coast road fortunately skirts around the city of **Algeciras**, typified by its busy port, smoky oil refineries and industrial suburbs. The road climbs steadily to the west, the mountainous landscape covered by literally thousands of creaking wind turbines. Look out for the Mirador del

Estrecho on the left-hand side of the road. There is a small shop, toilets and some stunning views of North Africa when the climatic conditions are right. This is also a good spot for observing the migration of raptors, particularly in spring when winds are blowing from the east. The road then descends to **Tarifa**. The word is said to mean 'wind' in Arabic and this is certainly the premier wind- and kitesurfing location in Europe. Tarifa itself is worth exploring, particularly the Moorish Castle. High-speed ferries leave here, arriving in Tangier 35 minutes later.

A few miles north of Tarifa is a side road that leads to the rather scruffy coastal village of **Bolonia**. The attraction here is the Roman ruins of Baelo Claudia. Dating from the late 2nd century, the town was important for the production of garum, a type of fish sauce that was highly prized in Rome. Old roads and shops are clearly marked and there is a small theatre, a forum and the remains of the vats where the garum was stored. Bolonia has a wide, windswept sandy beach that is usually deserted, apart from windsurfers and the local cattle and backed by half a dozen or so good seafood restaurants.

Further north is the small resort of **Zahara de los Atunes**, a name meaning 'blossom of the tuna fish'. Shoals of tuna migrate along the coast twice a year. They are herded into nets, hooked and hauled into boats – a dangerous business.

Vejer de la Frontera is a white town set on a hill above steep river cliffs. The old part of the town is

---

Cádiz
Distance from Gibraltar: 140 km (87 miles).
Cádiz Cathedral
⊠ Plaza de Catedral s/n, ☎ 956 259812, ⏱ Tue–Fri 10:00–14:00 and 16:30–19:30; Sat 10:00–13:00, Sun 11:00–13:00, 💰 entry fee includes museum.
Museo de Cádiz
⊠ Plaza de la Mina s/n, ☎ 956 212281, ⏱ Tue 14:30–20:00, Wed–Sat 09:00–20:00, Sun 09:30–13:00, 💰 entry fee for non-EU citizens.
Torre Tavira
⊠ C/Marques del Real Tesoro 10, ☎ 956 212910, ⏱ daily 10:00–18:00 (20:00 in summer), 💰 entry fee.

Opposite: The Alcazaba, Málaga's Moorish fortress.
Below: Tarifa is Spain's nearest city to Africa, and has a distinctive Arab flavour.

Ronda
Distance from Gibraltar: 118km (73 miles)
Tourist Information:
✉ Plaza de España 1,
☎ 952 871272, ⏰ Mon–Fri 09:00–19:30, Sat, Sun 10:00–14:00.
Baños Arabes Barrio de Padre Jesus, ☎ 952 873889, ⏰ Mar–Oct daily 10:00–19:00, Nov–Feb 10:00–18:00 Mon–Fri, Sat and Sun 10:00–15:00,
💰 admission charge with concessions.
Iglesia de Santa Maria Mayor, ✉ Plaza de Duquesa de Parcent s/n, ☎ 952 878653, ⏰ Apr–Oct 10:00–20:00, Nov–Mar 10:00–18:00 daily, 💰 admission charge with concessions.
Museo de Bandelero, ✉ Calle Armiñan 65, ☎ 952 877785, 🖥 www.museobandalero.com ⏰ Mar–Oct 10:30–20:30; Nov–Feb 10:30–18:30 daily, 💰 with concessions.
Casa de Mondragon, ✉ Plaza de Mondragon s/n, ☎ 952 878450, ⏰ Mar–Oct 10:00–19:00 Mon–Fri; Nov–Feb 10:00–18:00; Sat 10:00–15:00, 💰 with concessions.
Museo de Toros, ✉ Plaza de Toros Calle Virgen de la Paz 15, ☎ 952 871539, ⏰ Apr–Sep 10:00–20:00 daily, Mar–Oct 10:00–19:00 daily, Nov–Feb 10:00–18:00 daily, 💰 with concessions.

encircled by 15th century walls, through which Moorish gateways can be seen. Locate the parish church in Gothic/Mudéjar style and the 9th century Moorish castle, now converted into a house.

From Vejer, a road to the coast leads to the fishing port of **Barbate**, which has little to delay the visitor. Take the road eastwards through the forest of umbrella pines to Cape Trafalgar, the scene of the sea battle in 1805, where Nelson's fleet destroyed the combined French and Spanish navies. Sand dunes back the headland and blow into the little settlement of Los Caños de Meca, which has a strong alternative feel about it. To the north is **Conil de la Frontera**, a resort with a wide sandy beach and safe swimming, a favourite with Spanish families and, surprisingly, a number of prominent politicians.

Chiclana is a dormitory town of Cádiz with some light industry. On its coastal side is the rather garish resort area of **Novo Sancti Petri**, with its high-rise hotels and golf courses.

Marshland and salt pans signal the approach to **Cádiz**, situated on a long, narrow promontory, with the Bay of Cádiz to the east and the Atlantic Ocean on the west. The old part of the town is located on the tip of the peninsula. Cádiz is a 'one-off' as far as Andalucían cities are concerned. With a history going back to Phoenician times, it surprisingly short of monuments, due to the combined effects of earthquakes and buccaneers. Being a sea port it has been open to outside influences for centuries and as a result its people seem untypical of Andalucía, more tolerant and fun loving – characteristics that come the fore during the riotous *Carnaval* each February.

Don't miss the cathedral, with its twin gold domes. It replaced an earlier cathedral destroyed by fire and took from 1722 until 1822 to complete.

Ronda

For a true flavour of Spain, a visit to the ancient town of Ronda is hard to beat. It is a mere two-hour drive from Gibraltar. Take the coast road east and turn inland at San Pedro. From here, a well-engineered, scenic road winds up through forests emerging onto a high limestone plateau in the Serranía de Ronda mountains. The town sits astride a spectacular gorge – El Tajo – some 120m deep. Spanning the gorge are three bridges, the most impressive of which is the Puente Nuevo, completed in 1793. To the south of the bridge is the old town, with several features dating back to Moorish times, including the Baños Arabes (Moorish Baths). Much of the 13th-century structure remains intact and with recent renovation it makes an informative visit. The joy of Ronda, however, is simply wandering around the squares and narrow streets full of tall 18th century houses and sampling the many tapas bars. The Casa de Mondragon is the most important civil monument in Ronda. The one-time residence of Moorish princes and governors, it was adopted by the Christian monarchs Ferdinand and Isabella for their use as a palace, but it retains its Moorish arches, filigree work and fountain-filled patios. Today it functions as the town's social and archaeo-

Below: *The Puente Nuovo straddles the gorge at Ronda; it dates from 1793 and is the newest of the town's three bridges.*

EXCURSIONS

Banditry
Until recently, banditry was an acceptable occupation in Andalucía, where the rugged countryside was profitable territory for the brigand. Many of the bandits were Robin Hood-like characters, who stole from the rich, but made sure that the less fortunate in society were well looked after. The more privileged, however, were not so enamoured with the bandits and their protest led to the formation of the Civil Guard. Notorious bandits included José María Hinojosa Cobacho or 'El Tempranillo' and José Mingolla Gallardi, known to all and sundry as 'Pasos Largos' (Big Feet). Their exploits can be seen at Ronda in the Museo de Bandelero.

logical museum, with some excellent audio-visual displays, panoramas and walk-in caves. Another interesting museum in the old town is the Museo de Bandelero, which graphically describes the history of banditry in the Ronda mountains. The new part of the town, to the north of the Gorge, is dominated by the Plaza de Toros, built in 1785 and believed to be Spain's oldest bullring. Under the bullring is the Museo de Toros and whatever your feelings about bullfighting, this is a fascinating place, full of 'torobilia' such as photographs, posters, toreadors' clothing and bulls' heads, all with suitable background music. While in the newer part of Ronda, do find time to wander along the landscaped pathway, known as the Paseo de Blas Infante, with viewing terraces and vertiginous vistas over the gorge and the surrounding countryside.

Tangier

If you are on holiday in Gibraltar, it makes sense to take a quick trip across the Straits to the nearby continent of Africa. It couldn't be easier. Ferries leave from Gibraltar, Algeciras and Tarifa, high-speed catamarans from the latter taking a mere 35 minutes. Some ferries go to the Spanish enclave of Ceuta, but the usual destination is the city of Tangier, the summer capital of Morocco. During the first half of the 20th century, Tangier was a fashionable resort, popular with Europeans. Nearly half the population were expatriates, including at various times Barbara Hutton (the Woolworth heiress) and writers and artists such as Ian Fleming, Oscar Wilde and Francis Bacon, all attracted by the exotic atmosphere and perhaps its fame as a gay resort. At this time it also had a reputation for vice, but all

this had to change with the independence of Morocco in 1956. Today, Tangier has a rather down-at-heel look about it, resting on its former glories and notoriety, but it has all the ambience, sights and smells of a typical Arab town, making a ready contrast with Europe, just a few kilometres across the water.

Above: *Ceramic goods are just one of a variety of items that can be bought by visiting tourists.*

It is perfectly possible to travel to Morocco independently, but it is more convenient (and safer) for visitors to join an organized excursion. Most day trips to Tangier run by Gibraltar's travel agents, pick up their customers from their hotels and drive by coach to Tarifa, some 38km (24 miles) to the west. Here, the high-speed catamaran run by the FRS Line is boarded. The crossing gives the opportunity to watch the shipping in the Straits and observe sea birds such as gannets and shearwaters. On arriving at Tangier the visitors board a coach for a sightseeing tour of the city, including views of the Royal Palace and various embassies. There is also the dubious opportunity to take a ride on a camel. The tour then proceeds to the older part of Tangier for a guided walk around the souks, visiting a fruit and vegetable market, a carpet retail outlet and an herbalist. Visitors then have a traditional Moroccan meal with live music, before returning to the ship for the voyage back to Tarifa.

Beware of Hasslers
A major drawback of Tangier is the hassling of tourists, which can be heavy duty, constant and very skilled. If travelling independently it is best to go to the tourist office and hire an official guide, who will keep away the hasslers. However, remember that if you are accompanied by an official guide, you will pay an undeclared commission every time you purchase something.

RAGGED STAFF GATES

Above: *Ragged Staff Gates got their name from the crest of Charles V.*

Parking in Gibraltar

There are plenty of car parks in Gibraltar, but this doesn't mean parking is easy. You can pay for parking at the ICC car park in Line Wall Rd (this is multistorey and very convenient for the centre), at Queensway car park in Reclamation Road, at Europarking in Europort and at the airport car park. There is free parking at the Morrison's supermarket car park (but only for a limited period). Other free car parks include the Grand Parade by the cable car, but, frustratingly, this is almost permanently occupied by local residents, whose cars are only taken out at the weekends – some, in fact, seem to have their dust covers on for the duration!

Best Times to Visit

Gibraltar is an excellent all-year-round destination. **Winter** sees fewer holiday tourists and although there are some wet and windy days, the climate can be pleasantly mild and sunny. **Spring** is the best time for viewing the wild flowers and shrubs in the Upper Rock Nature Reserve. This season is also popular with bird-watchers, as raptors and storks will be migrating over the Rock on their northward journey from Africa. **Summer** can be hot, but Gibraltar will be refreshingly cooler than the nearby Costa del Sol. It is also the busiest time of the year, with full hotels and crowds thronging Main Street and visiting the attractions. This is the season that sees a number of cruise liners calling at the Rock. Expect long queues at the border during the summer months. **Autumn** can have very pleasant weather, but the first rains usually come during early October. Bird-watchers return in numbers during the autumn to see the southward migration of raptors.

Tourist Information

The main tourist office (and also the home of the Gibraltar Tourist Board) is at ⊠ Duke of Kent House,

Cathedral Square, opposite the Anglican Cathedral, ☎ 200 45000, 🖳 www.gibraltar.gov.uk ⊕ 09:00–17:30 Mon–Fri. There are also sub-offices in Casemates Square, the airport and at the docks when cruise liners are in port. There is an independent office in John Mackintosh Hall that has useful information. The Tourist Board have produced information sheets on such topics as history, geology and natural history. The only office maintained overseas is in London: Gibraltar Tourist Board, ✉ Arundel Great Court, 178/179 Strand, London, WC2R 1EL, ☎ 020 7836 0777, 📠 020 7240 6612.

Entry Requirements

A passport is needed to enter Gibraltar (or an ID card from certain EU countries). Delays at the border are notorious, depending on the prevailing attitude of the Spanish customs. Allow half an hour if crossing by car. Pedestrians are normally waved straight through, so it makes sense to leave a car on the Spanish side of the border. In any case, car parking in Gibraltar can be a nightmare (*see panel page 84*).

Customs

Gibraltar is a duty-free territory and as such is not considered part of the EU from the point of view of customs allowances. The following restrictions apply:
• 200 cigarettes or 50 cigars or 250g (8oz) of pipe tobacco.
• 2 litres still table wine plus 1 litre spirits or liqueur
• 60 ml (2 fluid ounces) perfume
• Other goods valued to £145.
Restrictions apply on the import of other items, including firearms, protected species, meat products and pets. There are no restrictions on currency.

Health Requirements

No vaccinations are required.

Getting There

By air: At present, the only European flights in and out of Gibraltar are to and from the UK. The 'no frills' airline **easyJet** (who recently took over GB Airways, once a subsidiary of British Airways and a long-standing operator of Gibraltar flights) runs daily flights from London Gatwick; UK reservations: ☎ 0905 821 0905, 🖳 www.easyjet.com **British Airways** also operates daily flights from London Gatwick; UK reservations: ☎ 084577 333 77, 🖳 www.britishairways.com **Monarch Airlines** runs daily flights from London Luton and twice-weekly flights from Manchester; UK reservations ☎ 08700 405040, 🖳 www.monarch.co.uk All three airlines have offices at Gibraltar airport. Flight time from the UK is around two and a half hours. There has long been friction with Spain over Gibraltar airport regarding the inability of Spanish airlines to use the facility. This ended in 2006 as part of the Córdoba Agreement. **Iberia** then set up a regular service between Gibraltar and Madrid, but ironically this route was dropped, due to lack of custom. A popular alternative is to use Málaga airport in Spain, some 120km (75 miles) to the east, and to proceed to Gibraltar by coach or hired car. Málaga can be reached from a large number of regional airports in the UJK and a number of other European countries. Gibraltar airport is unusual in that it is within walking distance from the town centre and also that the runway crosses Winston Churchill Avenue, the main north-south street. Traffic has to stop when aircraft land or take off. This difficulty should be overcome when a road tunnel is opened, possibly in late 2009 or early 2010.

By Public Transport: La Línea is linked to other towns in Andalucía by efficient coach services, with buses from Málaga, Estepona, Granada, Seville and Jerez. There are also long-distance coaches from Barcelona and Madrid. The main operating companies are Portillo (☎ 956 172396) and Comes (☎ 956 170093). There is a direct, if slow, train line from Algeciras to Madrid. Another line runs from Ronda to Algeciras. For information ☎ 902 240202. Visitors to Gibraltar arriving at Málaga airport will find a train service running from the airport to Fuengirola. From here there are four buses a day to La Linea. There are also direct buses running from Málaga airport to La Línea at roughly one-hour intervals.

Money Matters

The currencies in Gibraltar are the Gibraltar pound and the pound sterling, which are interchangeable. Euros can be used in shops, but not in the post office, and remember that Gibraltar currency cannot be used in Spain. Ask for your change in Euros if you are going back over the border. There are numerous banks, usually branches of the main British and Spanish organizations. They are mainly to be found in Main Street and all have ATMs. Banks are open between 09:00 and 15:30 Mon–Fri. There are also numerous exchange bureaux, which open longer hours. There is a series of Gibraltar crowns which can be purchased in some of the souvenir shops in Main

Street and sets of current coinage are also available from the main post office.

Travellers' Cheques: You will need your passport when changing travellers' cheques. Commission is usually charged. Banks offer the best rates.

Credit Cards: Most hotels, shops and restaurants accept the major international credit cards.

VAT: As a duty-free zone, Gibraltar has no value added tax on goods bought in shops.

Tipping: Check if a service charge is added to bills in restaurants. If it is, there is no need to tip, despite the blank space left for tipping on credit card counterfoils. Otherwise a tip of 10–15% might be paid for good service. Taxi drivers and tour guides will expect a tip.

Transport

Bringing a car into Gibraltar is a dubious advantage, because of the delays at the border crossing and the difficulty in parking. If you are a day visitor to Gibraltar, it is best to leave your car on the Spanish side of the border and take one of the frequent buses, which run at 15-minute intervals from the border into town. Buses also run around the town and out to Europa Point, linking many of the tourist attractions. The tourist offices have timetables. A taxi is another possibility. The 1.5km (0.93-mile) walk into town is quite entertaining as it involves crossing the airport runway. If you are staying in Gibraltar for a few nights you will find that most of the hotels have some form of parking arrangements. Visitors who need to take their cars onto the Rock will find that the queues from the border post stretch along the waterfront at La Linea for several hundred yards and at peak times you can queue for up to an hour. Remember that driving is on the right, the same as in Spain. To take a car into Gibraltar, you will need an insurance certificate, registration document, nationality plate and a valid driving licence, although in fact these are rarely checked.

Business Hours

Shops are normally open from 09:00 until 19:30, without the siesta closure found in neighbouring Spain. They usually close at 13:30 on Saturdays and are closed all day on Sunday, although some tourist sites may open every day. Most other businesses and offices will close at 17:30.

Time Difference

Both Spain and Gibraltar are one hour ahead of the UK. The clocks go forward in the last week of March and back again in the last week in October.

Communications

Post: the main post office is located at 104 Main Street, open Mon–Fri 09:00–13:00 and 14:00–17:00, Sat 10:00–13:00. They don't accept Euros. Gibraltar issues its own postage **stamps**. Stamps can also be bought in many shops, particularly those selling postcards. A wide range of philatelic services are available, such as first-day covers and presentation packs. Contact the Gibraltar Philatelic Bureau Ltd. ✉ Po Box 5662, Gibraltar, ☎ (350) 75662 📠 (350) 42149.

Telephones: In Gibraltar, telephones have traditionally had five-digit numbers, but in September 2008 the prefix 200 was introduced, giving eight-digit numbers. To dial Gibraltar from abroad, dial the international access code (00) followed by Gibraltar's country code (350) and then the local eight-digit number. When phoning from the Costa del Sol or the rest of Spain, use the prefix 9567 and then the local number. To make a call abroad from Gibraltar, dial the international access code, followed by the country code, area code and number. When phoning the UK, miss out the zero at the start of the area code. In Gibraltar, you can make international as well as local calls from street payphones. Some country codes include Australia 61, USA and Canada 1, New Zealand 64, Ireland 353, France 33, Singapore 65, Hong Kong 852, South Africa 27 and UK 44. Mobile phones generally work well in Gibraltar, using the local provider Gibtel or the Spanish providers Airtel or Movistar (a number of shops sell cheap mobile phones which can be discarded after your visit). Telephone cabins in Gibraltar are of the traditional British red version.

Internet Access: General Internet Business Centre, ✉ 36 Governor's Street, ☎ 200 44227, 🕐 10:00–22:00 Tue–Sat, 12:00–21:00 Sun–Mon. Small charge per hour. Café Cyberworld, ✉ Units 14–16, Ocean Heights Gallery, Fishmarket Road, ☎ 200 51416, 🕐 12:00 to midnight daily. Small charge per hour. Many of the hotels also provide Internet access.

Broadcasting Services: Radio Gibraltar, daily 06:45–24:00 in English and Spanish; CBC-TV, programme details in local papers. Free weekly programme sheet available from tourist offices.

Health Precautions

No special health precautions, injections or vaccinations are necessary for Gibraltar, or for excursions to

Spain and North Africa. EU citizens should be in possession of an EHIC (European Health Insurance Card), which allows reciprocal health arrangements should you need treatment at a public hospital. This is no substitute, however, for a good travel insurance that provides medical cover. There are nine pharmacies in Gibraltar, the majority in Main Street. There is also a Health Centre in ✉ Casemates Square, ☎ 200 72355, offering 24-hour emergency facilities, while the new St Bernard's Hospital, ☎ 200 79700, built on reclaimed land located near the port, also provides 24-hour emergency cover. Treatment is free for EU nationals, but there is a small charge for prescribed medicines. Tap water is safe to drink, but many Gibraltarians prefer bottled water.

Emergencies

In an emergency dial ☎ 199 for police or an ambulance. The main police headquarters is at ✉ New Mole House, Rosia Road, ☎ 200 72500. There is another police station at ✉ 120 Irish Town, ☎ 200 72500. The police In Gibraltar wear British-style uniforms and are generally approachable and helpful.

Useful Websites

🖥 www.gibraltar.gi
🖥 www.gibraltar.gov.uk or 🖥 www.gibraltar.gov.gi The official site maintained by the government of Gibraltar, 🖥 www.mygibraltar.co.uk (useful for booking hotels and tours.)
🖥 www.gibnet.com
🖥 www.gibraltar.com For information on neighbouring parts of Spain, visit 🖥 www.andalucia.com and 🖥 www.andalucia.org

Electricity

Electric current is the same as in Britain – 220V or 240V with plugs of three flat pins. Most American or European appliances will need an adaptor. Most airport shops usually sell these adaptors.

Weights and Measures

Imperial measurements have now been replaced with metric in line with the rest of Europe.

Personal Safety

Gibraltar must be one of the safest places in the world and the visitor is more likely to be mugged or robbed by a Barbary ape than by a fellow human being. With just one tightly controlled border crossing, a criminal could only leave the Rock by boat. Nevertheless it is wise to use common sense and take the following precautions: Don't carry more cash than you need for the day. Keep your wallet or purse out of sight. Never leave a handbag or luggage unattended. Avoid poorly lit areas at night. Women travellers will be perfectly safe in Gibraltar. Male machismo is confined to the other side of the border!

Disabled Access

A number of tourist sites in Gibraltar, particularly on the Upper Rock, have difficult access or restricted geography for wheelchairs. These include St Michael's Caves, the Great Siege Tunnels, the Cable Car and the Alameda Wildlife Park. Many of the bastions and gun emplacements present similar difficulties. The authorities are aware of the problems, but hope that handicapped people will appreciate that many of the sites are difficult to adapt. The John Mackintosh Hall has good access, with lifts to the first floor, but the Museum has access to the lower floor only. There are disabled user spaces in all of Gibraltar's car parks, but badge holders should not park on double yellow lines. The public toilets all have facilities for disabled users. Hotel facilities for the disabled vary greatly. Some have rooms specifically for the disabled, others recommend a companion to accompany wheelchair users during their stay. The O'Callaghan Elliott Hotel has obtained a Disability Friendly Award and is centrally located. The Cannon Hotel has no facilities for the disabled, as all rooms are located on the first floor and there are no lifts. Handicapped tourists should contact individual hotels or the Gibraltar Tourist authorities for information prior to booking accommodation. There is also useful information on 🖥 www.disability.gi **Shopmobility Centre**, ✉ Unit G4B, International Commercial Centre, Casemates Square, ☎ 200 79898, ⏱ 09:30–13:00 and 14:00–17:00. Closed weekends. Bookings can be made one day in advance and a passport is required as a deposit.

Etiquette

Like other Mediterranean countries, Gibraltar is an easy-going place with few formal dress codes anywhere. Shorts are quite acceptable in the summer months. At Gibraltar's beaches and hotel pools, topless sunbathing is unusual, but tolerated. Like their fellow British, the Gibraltarians are believers in queueing and don't take kindly to those not prepared to stand in line for their turn. Unlike in other Mediterranean countries, and despite the cheap cigarettes available on the Rock, smoking has become less acceptable in public places, hotels and public transport.

Gay and Lesbian Travellers

The gay scene is almost non-existent on the Rock, although there is plenty of activity for gay people over the border in Spain, particularly in Cádiz and Marbella (see Entertainment).

Concessions

There are usually concessions available for children and the elderly. Note that museums in Spain should provide free entry for citizens of EU countries.

Consular Services

Belgium, ✉ 47 Irish Town, ☎ 200 78353, 📠 200 77383, ⌨ pimossi@smith/imossi.gi

Denmark, ✉ Cloister Building, Market Lane, ☎ 200 76821, 📠 200 71608.

Finland, ✉ 20 Line Wall Rd, ☎ 200 75149, 📠 200 70513.

France, ✉ PO Box 135, 209/204 Main Street, ☎ 200 78830, 📠 200 75867.

Greece, ✉ 47 Irish Town, ☎ 200 73500.

Iceland, ✉ 123 Main Street (3rd floor), ☎/📠 200 47096, ⌨ anne.lundin@danish-alteriors.com

Israel, ✉ Marine View, Glacis Rd, ☎ 200 77735, 📠 200 74301.

Italy, ✉ PO Box 437, 3/1 Irish Place, ☎/📠 200 47096.

Latvia, ✉ 3 Parliament Lane, ☎ 200 75688.

Netherlands, ✉ Suite 9.1, ICC Main Street, ☎ 200 79220, 📠 200 78512.

Norway, ✉ Regal house, Queensway, ☎ 200 79620, 📠 200 45994.

Poland, ✉ 35 Governor's Parade, ☎ 200 74593.

Russia, ✉ Suite 8743a, Europort, ☎ 200 51070, 📠 200 51032.

Sweden, ✉ Cloister Building, Irish Town, ☎ 200 72663, 📠 200 76189.

Thailand, ✉ 120 Main Street, ☎ 200 46315/78301.

Visitors to Gibraltar

The tourist market to Gibraltar is largely based on short-stay breaks, calls from cruise liners and yachts and, more significantly, day-trip tourism from visitors from Spain. For instance, over 8 million persons are estimated to cross the land frontier annually, while a mere 125,000 arrive by air. The cruise trade grows by the year and it is estimated that in 2009 there will be 237 cruise liner calls with a total number of 356,000 passengers. Little wonder that a new cruise terminal has been built. A recent development is the expansion of Gibraltar as a conference destination, with several hotels providing corporate facilities.

Gibraltar's Main Tourist Office

The main tourist office in Bomb House Lane is located in a building full of interest. It is known as **Line Wall House** and until quite recently was used as the Fortress Headquarters. It was also once an officers' mess. It was rebuilt from ruins after the Great Siege and again after a fire in 1833. Prince George of Cambridge lived here in 1838 and later it was the residence of the General Officer commanding the Royal Artillery.

INDEX OF SIGHTS

General Index

GENERAL INDEX

General Index

GENERAL INDEX